RED INK OF BLOOD

ALAN HINES

 www.trafford.com
North America & international
toll-free: 1 888 232 4444 (USA & Canada)
fax: 812 355 4082

Acknowledgements: Thank you Heavenly Father
for blessing me to live to see another day.

Thank all for all your many blessings. Thank you for
blessing me to have my grandmother, Jean Hines, and my
mother Joyce Hines as a part of my life, may they rest in
peace. Thanks to everyone that showed me any kind of
support on previous books, God Bless everybody...This
book is not suitable for viewers under the age of 18.

BOOKS OF POETRY ALREADY PUBLISHED BY ALAN HINES,

1. Reflections of Love
2. Thug Poetry Volume 1
3. The Words I Spoke
4. Joyce
5. Constant Visions
6. Red Ink of Blood

URBAN NOVEL ALREADY PUBLISHED BY ALAN HINES,

1. Book Writer
2. Queen of Queens

UPCOMING BOOKS OF POETRY BY ALAN HINES,

1. Reflections of Love (Volume 2,and 3)
2. This is Love (Volume 1, 2, and 3)
3. Founded Love (Volume 1,2, and 3)
4. True Love (Volume 1,2,and 3)
5. Love (Endless Volumes)
6. Tormented Tears (Volume 1,2,and 3)
7. A Inner Soul That Cried (Volume 1,2,and 3)
8. Visionary (Endless Volumes)
9. In My Eyes To See (Volume 1,2, and 3)
10. A Seed That Grew (Volume 1,2,and, 3)
11. The Words I Spoke (Volume 2,and 3)
12. Scriptures (Volume 1,2, and 3)
13. Revelations (volume 1,2, and 3)
14. Destiny (Volume 1,2, and 3)
15. Trials and Tribulations (Volume 1,2, and 3)
16. IMMORTALITY (Volume 1,2, and 3)
17. My Low Spoken Words (Volume 1,2, and 3)
18. Beauty Within (Volume 1,2, and 3)
19. Red Ink of Blood (Volume 1,2, and 3)
20. Destiny of Light (Jean Hines) (Volume 1,2, and 3)
21. Deep Within (Volume 1, 2, and 3)
22. Literature (Volume 1, 2, and 3)

23. Silent Mind (Volume 1,2, and 3)
24. Amor (Volume 1,2, and 3)
25. Joyce (Volume 1,2, and 3)
26. Lovely Joyce (Volume 1,2, and 3)
27. Pink Lady (Volume 1,2, and 3)
28. Mockingbird Lady (Volume 1,2, and 3)
29. Godly tendicies (Volume 1,2, and 3)
30. Enchanting Arrays (Volume 1,2, and 3)
31. Harmony (Volume 1,2, and 3)
32. Realism (Volume 1,2, and 3)
33. Manifested Deep Thoughts (Volume 1,2, and 3)
34. Poectic Lines of Scrimage (Volume 1,2, and 3)
35. Garden of Love (Volume 1,2, and 3)
36. Reflection In The Mirror. (Volume 1,2, and 3)

UPCOMING NON-FICTION BOOKS BY ALAN HINES,

1. Time Versus Life
2. Timeless Jewels
3. The Essence of Time
4. Memoirs of My Life
5. In my Eyes To See
6. A Prisoner's Black History

UPCOMING URBAN NOVELS BY ALAN HINES,

1. Black Kings
2. Playerlistic
3. The Police
4. Scandalous
5. The West Side Rapist
6. Shattered Dreams
7. She Wrote Murder
8. Black Fonz
9. A Slow Form of Suicide
10. No Motherfucking Love
11. War Stories
12. Storm

1. GOD'S REASON

God's reason for me breathing is to spread
wealth and goodness breeding.
Shine throughout the four seasons.
Give guidance in leading.
Sacrifice my life for others as nourishment for hunger feeding.
Tell the truth in which I believe in.
Be more interested in giving than receiving.
God's reason for me breathing is to give others life meaning.

2. TOMMY DREAMER

Dreamed of dreams.
Wanted to be king of kings.
Wanted to take away his own addiction of being a fiend.
Selling dreams, sold schemes.
Had women thinking they were queens.
Even in the midst of soap he wasn't clean.
Did his own thing.
Hustling people for a little change.
He dreamed of one day being on the movie screen,
the cover of magazines.
Wanted fans to scream his name.
Tommy Dreamer had big dreams.
But loved the dope as it seems.
Chase the dope like a fiend.
Would smoke crack and go into a world of dreams.
Felt periodic signs of a emperor,
ambassador or a king.
But in reality Tommy was a dopefiend with dreams.
Tommy Dreamer, dreamed.

3. THAT'S A LOW DOWN DIRTY SHAME

Majority of his life was wasted using heroic heroin,
and rocked cocaine.
Had no shame in his game.
He let it be what it was and did his thing.
Started off early serving in the game,
and even then came money and fame.
Eventually he wanted to try new things.
First started snorting just a little bit of cocaine,
and then graduated into a higher peddle, gold medal heroin,
and rocked cocaine.
In time his attitude and ways of living changed.
Things happen in the game, some I can't explain,
but his money became foreign and strange.
In due time he was a true fiend that told stories,
about ancient things, when he once had everything.
Right now today he's a addicted fiend, for it do anything.
Kids, and grandkids don't even know
him, don't even know his name.

Who am I to judge or call bad names,
but that's a low down dirty shame to forever be a drug fiend.

4. ABOUT

It's all about love and respect.
Those with guns, and will use them to protect.
Who shall really stand by your side under the threat of death.
In times of trials and errors who will accept calls of collect;
away from home show love, and respect,
not saying but actually doing
this and that.
Most gracious a traditional fest.
Love that will never ignore, and always respect.
Being true, flaws accept.....
It's all about love and respect.

5. Highest Degree

Seasons greetings,
even when it wasn't the holiday seasons.
Loved my poetry readings.
In the bedroom wanted to be pleasing.
My child she wanted to be breeding.
My love forever she was seeking.
Told me all her secrets even things she did
with others under the sheets.
Genuinely she wanted our love to forever be.
She said I made her life complete.
She made it a treat everytime we'd meet.
She treated me like I wore the crown as she got
on her knees with an aim to please.
She made each day like the holiday season as
she loved me to the highest degree.

6. STAINED MIRROR

It was a stain in the mirror,
but yet and still she could see things clearer.
No Pilgrims or Happy Thanksgiving, but
instead roaches that fell from ceilings.
Gun shots of killings.
Abandon buiding living.
Mices that walked around as if they rented.
Kris Kringle ponded gifts on Christmas.
She'd bare witness to those that got high as the
only way to achieve a wonderful prism.
Over packed prisons of those that didn't listen,
didn't abide be the fundamental
written guidance of the literature.
She'd seen those before her that made wrong
decisions, she'd let that be a lesson
learned off others failed missions.
Those that's telling the ones secretly planted kisses.
Obituarys of those we love R.I.P. we miss them.
Lives that was confiscated over foolish and petty issues.
She blanked out and broke all mirrors, more
then seven years bad luck superstition
would definitely continue.
Took a piece of the broken mirror and slid both of her wrist tissue,
couldn't live the life of reality of a stain mirror.

7. ADVANCE PLANING

Advancements, and large numbered royalties I'm seeking.
Gotta leave my past behind,
the love of romance for the streets.
Twins, and N'dia my love is to keep;
thou shall always feed, already know what you need.
I'm a guide, teach, and lead, my love is always unto thee.

8. WRITING BOOKS

In chase and pursuit of a happiness
of success that's long over due.
Awaiting a dream come true.
Self made guru;
but I do what I do.
Manuscripts on top of manuscripts, some old some new.
Each day learning, earning currency due.
It's some hard work but I know success will
come to life through the truth,
once God feel like the time is due.....

9. PLEASURE OF PAIN

She enjoyed the pleasure of pain.
She loved playing sexual war games.
She loved yelling my name as she made me mad I forced it all the
way in her gave her everything;
she'd make me mad on purpose so she
could feel the pleasure of pain.
She'd love how in the bedroom I'd mistreat
her and call her the females dog name.

I honestly believe I treated her the same as
the rest that had went and came.
But to her our relationship was everything,
in the bedroom I made it rain.

11. Mental Disasters

Mental pics of my own self laying dead in a casket.
Killed by a teenager that had no father,
no parental guidance, he was a dirty bastard.

Mental pics of me being a slave,
and having to call another human being master,
what a disaster.

Menatal pics of me being in the midst of the dragon,
the beast empire doing sinful works being yelled at to do it faster.

Mental pics of me being stuck in a mental institution,
seeing illusions, confusion.

A prison of disaster, everlasting.

Souls that shall get eternal life in hell,
burn in eternal fire.
Drugs that took people higher.
A socialism of Pinocchio's liars and evilness of
preaching pastors.....
Mental images of disaster.

12. LADY LIGHT

Lady light what a sight of delight.
Craved to see you even in the darkest nights.
She brought things to the light, to life.
Kept it tight.
Did the things I liked.
Listened when I was right.
But remained silent as the poetry I write.
She said my poems should be recited over the open mic.
She said she loved making love in the bed each night.....
She shined so bright, lady light.

13. RUSH

They all told me, "slow down your in a rush enjoy your life you
work, and write books entirely to much."
I didn't listen because I wanted success to be lived up.
I wanted to be a boss that owned, possess lots of stuff.
While everyone else was at fiestas living it up,
I was either at work or at home writing poetry, music, and novels in
which I love, I lust.
I know dedication and hard work comes
those green and white papers
that say in God We Trust.
It was like an adrenline rush as direct
deposits had became grown ups.
I seen others that wanted but didn't own up.
I did positively in a rush so that check
to check living wouldn't even
come up, each new book would be a plus, and
success through me for we, for us
would come quick fast in a hurry, in a rush.

14. UNLIMITED EDITION

An edition of bodies that mysteriously came
up missing.
Poor kids that will never see Christmas.
Over packed prisons.
New crimes, and new laws being invented.
Those that's free with sick intentions.
Stressed out over bad decisions.
Ponds of drowning kids, dead bodies ate by vicious fishes.
Real life superstition.
Painful bodies filled with staples and stiches.
A real life unlimited edition in which we must live in
suspended until the creator officially says it's finish.

15. FACE REALITY

Face to face with reality.
Wars of casulties.
Segregated families.
A cheating spouses mentality.
Finding a decent salary.
Third worlds poverty.
A repeating of time of protesting against racism gallery.
And at the end of life we all must die tragicly.
Reality.

16. CLOCK

I'd sit and watch the clock wondering when
the madness and chaos would stop.
As the youth get killed by the flocks.
Shell shocked hearing gun shots that just wont stop.
Wishing I had the have nots.
Constantly being caught on tape, crooked cops.
Getting older with age as time repeats never stops.
Eventually my casket shall drop.
Father of time, clock never stops,
as I reminisce and continue to watch.

17. DREAMS

Sometimes things are, sometimes things aint what they seem,
nothing comes to a dreamer but a dream;
guess who told me that, a dopefiend.
At that point in time I didn't understand what she'd mean.
She meant that a sleeper that dreams will
never live out their dreams to achieve
success and earn cream,
they got to get up spread wings, and breathe, and do things.
Eyes wide open, and seen, living out dreams.

18. BUYING TIME

Doctor's appointments,
exercising,
standing in health care lines.
As deaths are continiously inclined.
Leaving family members and friends behind.
Steady dying.
Never knowing who's next in line.
Never knowing when it's your time.
In reality we're living to dying.

19. LONGING

I want, and long for you.
Wanted to be right, not wrong for you.
I want to be with you.
Giving you a love that you could never come by or even close to.
I even wrote a song for you.
Our love will always be true.....
All along I long for you.

20. COURAGE

Courage and sight.
Power in life.
Worshipping God and his son Jesus Christ.
Will and might.
Studying and striving for better days and nights.
Not with a sword but with a pen winning all fights.

21. THANKS GOD

Thanks God for always be there before I
was even old enough to know you.
Thanks for being the only one there when rent is due.
Thanks God for at my older age making my feel brand new.
Thanks God for helping me live out my dreams
that hasn't yet totally came true;
thanks for giving me a pen, a paper to write
poetry to make the gray skies turn blue.
Thanks God for forever being true.
Thanks God for simply just being you.

22. TRAGIC LOST

A tragic lost.
From project windows infants and little kids was tossed;
by those whom hearts had turned frost.
From dealers, what their mom's loved was bought.
Souls were sold to the Devil for a low cost.
Street wars and murder cases were caught.
Some took it to trial, beyond a reasonable doubt,
they lost.
And the process continues from east, west,
north, south.....
Tragic lost.

23. NO SUBSTITUTION {JEAN HINES}

She came with no substitution.
No New Years resolution,
her everything was to use the power of
prayer as her guide of movement.
She abided by each scripture Dueteronomy,
Psalms and Proverbs including.....
Everything I did she'd encourage me to strive for improvement.
She prayed that one day I'd graduate as a college student.
Her love was so wonderful, and so soothing.
She was against domestic violence, and child abusing.
Fifteen kids, loved God, an abortion clinic would never use it.
As time keep manuevoring could never find another her,
not even a substitution.....

24. WELL {JEAN HINES}

I knew that you meant well.
You sent money orders and prayed for those
that rotted in jail cells.
You told people to try harder after they failed.
The anointing of blessing oil, and the kingdom
of the Lord to come was the story you'd tell.
You loved all and wished them well.
Gave everything to church offerings in person
and through the mail.
Turned good out of the freshes things that had once went stale.
A sweet scent was your natural smell.
God Bless in Heaven you made it, you dwell.
I love you, and I wish you well.

25. LADY BLUES

This lady would sing the blues.
At a slow yet stylistic groove,
while being entertain by instrumental tools.
She'd speak her mind, felt as she had nothing to loose.
Pouring her heart out in the form of blues.
Sometimes that's all she'd do.
And I loved and adored her groove,
she was cool.
Dedicated to me she'd sing songs of blues telling me I love you.
And I loved her to.
A guru that song the blues.

26. GREATFUL OF BLESSINGS

Our father whom are in Heaven,
I appreciate your continuous blessings,
even the times when I was stressing,
you put me through that so I could learn valuable lessons.
Although I haven't been to church in a while I still try
to do righteous stepping.
No sins of sick sinful confessions.
To me your greater than any gift, jewel, or presents.....
The only Lord of Lords, King of Kings, the
almighty Heavenly Father of blessings.

27. STUCK

Stuck in a cave.
Trapped in a maze,
a permanent daze.
Overlays for the rotten under plays.
Painful memories that never fade.
Stuck, stuck in time, a cave, a phase, a worldwide maze.

28. A Pimp

I pimp my pen so it could write.
I pimp my pen so it could give the dead and the old a new life.
I pimp my pen so spectators could see
visions of sky rockets in flight,
as a sense of delight.
I pimp my pen so it could do the things I like.
I pimp my pen so it could go out and get me that money
throughout the days and weary nights, through amazon.com,
and other cites.
I pimped, I pimped my pen so it could write.

29. LOVE BEING

Love being dispursed.
Undid a bad spell, of a curse.
A caring for me sickness, as a nurse.
She loved me which was the truth,
felt good didn't hurt.
Genuine love that was always being dispured.....
Stray bullet hit her, had to bury her six feet under the dirt;
I wonder if she'd make it to the Heavens above the Earth.
Her love shall forever be dispursed.

30. REALITY CHECK

Reality came through like trying to cash a bad check.
Hot flashes and constant regrets,
problems can't forget.

Breaking necks,
popping tecs for respect.
Blacks gotta watch their backs for those that's assinged and paid
salaries to serve and protect.

Shell shocked street warrior vets.
Sexual predators that sweat.
No places of peace to rest within humanly flesh until death.

And when it's all said and done no one shall live forever,
one day we all must be laid to rest.....Reality check.

31. LOVELY SPARKS

A shining in the dark.
A enlightment that sparked.
A love in heart.
A alienated superstar had to be from outerspace like Mars.
A freedom from shackles, chains, and bars.
A lovely spark like fireworks in nights filled with dark.
A lovely spark.

32. I Opened

I opened my eyes and instantly seen the sunrise.
Seen Jesus lifting up souls to Heaven right in front of my eyes.
Seen the ancient profits doing their things
as they preached the word
of God as they baptized.
A final place of peace for those that died.
I shall forever lend a helping hand do away with foolish pride.
Avoid and dodge trouble that lies.
Try to achieve greatness of the best kind,
leaving the past behind,
using the God giving smartness in my mind.
I opened my eyes and seen the righteous
path as the Lord is my guide.

33. MOTIVATIONAL TOOL

A motivational tool, my quest to improve.
To myself everything to gain, and prove, nothing to lose.
Road down bumpy roads on my way to ships that cruise.
A life that was a gift giving as a motivational tool to
be the most improved student like in grammer school,
so I could conquer a quest and someday rule.

34. I Awoke

I awoke to the choking of smoke;
seen through it that life just wasn't a joke.
Watching my back for the peoples and the folks.
Bear witness to the youth strung out on dope.
Reminisce to myself on how blacks was punished
by being hung on ropes.

35. Destruct

In a land of destructive hanging ropes.
People using my hallway so they could smoke.
Violent acts being committed only because
the aggressor was provoked.

I awoked knowing it'll be me by myself when
times get hard as the weather turns
cold.
Running through a maze not knowing which way to go.

I awoke reading my own book of life in which I lived in and wrote.

36. WRONG ROUTES

Took a road that was the wrong route within fate.
Instead of being an attorney fighting cases, chose the wrong route
in and out of police station, no money stacked
using a public defender to beat cases.
No outdates face to face with the judge and the state.
Black on black crimes, and then you got the police that racist.
Officials being defaced, pleasant memories were erased.
At an old age no 401k, no success had came to
stay, reality rained on each ordinary
day.
Made foolish decisions took wrong routes, led astray.

37. UNDERSTANDING

Knowledge, wisdom, and understanding.
A process of being demanding.
Being uncanning.
Uncertainly of stunts, outlanding.
Thinking ahead and planning.
Being aware of surroundings still standing.
Obeying things within each glance.
Seperating your inner boy into a man.
Living life prosperous through studying, thinking, working hard,
utilizing knowledge, wisdom, and understanding.

38. WONDER

A wonderful feeling,
worth millions.
A beautiful, peaceful environment to
live in.
No senseless killings,
or dope sells from abandon buildings.
Never dying forever living.
No poor, money to the ceiling.
Oh what a wonderful feeling.
A wonderful world to live in.
And then I woke up out a dream to Satan's dealings.

39. LOVE EVERLASTING

I love you more than anything.
My everything.
Addicted like a fiend.
I'm your king, you're my queen.
Love hot as steam.
It's as it came true from a dream.
Even my kids that aren't biologically yours feel the
love and everything.
Seeing us together makes others hearts and minds sing.
To me our love should be everlasting it should be everything.

40. PROJECTED VISIONS

Projected visions of better living.
No battles with Indians, and Pilgrims,
Happy Thanksgiving.
Appeals being granted, they coming home from prison.
Love and assistance.
Happily, faithfully married Mr. and Mrs.
And then we all raise children to live life successfully and
prosperous in which was giving.

41. WAS LIKE

She was like a righteous Catholic priest.
A Goddess of the streets.
In the bed she let me do me,
she allowed me to be free,
realistic pornography I did see.
But through it all she kept it one hundred, complete.
Around her is where I always wanted to be.
she abided by the the rule that I wore the pants,
she wore the panties.
Our conversations of progress was endlessly.
She was like my soul mate to be.
A special part of me.
Tranquility I did see.
She was so good to me.

42. SIGHT IN THE DARKEST OF NIGHT

In the darkest night is when I see sight.
The rebirth of Jesus Christ.
Peace treaties being sign no wars, or fights.
While everybody is at a Fiesta I'm in the lab
creating masterpieces of delight;
in which I love to write, knowing someday
royalties payments will sky rocket to
a prestiges height.

In the darkest night I have the ability to
seperate wrong from rights.
A non-existence of foolish pride.
Letting Lucifer's whispering in my ear be
done with, relinquish, and die.

In the darkest night I pick up my pen,
and write to give a vision, a sight.

43. WITHOUT SHE

Without she I couldn't see.
Without she I couldn't be free.
Without she I couldn't even be me.
Without she I'd be incomplete,
without she.

44. DON'T BITE

Don't bite that apple you open up doors
for others to prey and scheme on you for survival.

Don't bite that apple smell it, it's more fishier than Perch or
Red Snapple, images of allys when they all are rivals.

Please don't bite that apple you'll forever be in debt
saying to yourself I did it again a repeating
cycle of getting the same results
with different people in significant times of trying.

45. CORRUPT

In a land that has already self destruct, corrupt
praying that the Lords blessings go up.
It's to late same gender lust.
Lust to much for one another to love and touch.
Gang bangers constantly breeding and tossing it up.
Out of luck;
in prison like slaves inmates are stuck,
in a system that's unjust and corrupt.
Battles and knives daily people are being struct.
By living in a land that has already self destruct, corrupt.

46. One In The Same

We're one in the same writing poetry as a
freeful spirited way to maintain.
Together we'd bow our heads and pray in Jesus name.
To the both of us loyalty, honor, and respect was everything.
King and queen.
A shining love that gleamed.
A came true dream that the both us had seen.
My everything, a beautiful human being.
Positive minds that was on the same thing;
the growth and develpment for children to prosper, be educated,
and live out dreams.
Craving for a world without fiends.
I loved just hearing her name,
I truly believe she felt mutual, the same.
It's strange but I hope our love will never change,
stay the same.
One in the same, she be my everything.

47. FLY

She wanted to fly, how high?
She wanted to soar like a bald Eagle in the sky.
She wanted to reach her highest peek of
accomplishing goals to acheive;
to teach the world to sing in perfect harmony.

She wanted to fly so high to see Heaven in her eyes;
souls with eternal life.
Face to face with the sun as it rise.

She wanted to fly touch the sky,
live forever with no reason why living
forever without having to die.

She wanted to touch the sky, acheive greatness at it's all time high.

48. CAME

Reality came in the form of tears right after the judge
sentence him to a hundred percent of 75 years.
Wishing the judge and state would die having no more life to live.
Knowing that the witnesses would be buried
in caskets as their family and
friends shed tears.
He got back to his cell constantly repeating,"
I'm not suppose to be here."
Shattered his dreams of freedom coming near.
In cells he must spend Christmas and New Years.
Trial with witnesses should've never appeared;
to him the end of the world was here.
Must spend all that time in prison.....75 years.

49. AFTER ALL

After all she had love that was gigantic
instead of small.
She gave love in it's entirety, it's all.
Made me stand tall throughout it all.
Would be there to catch me if I ever stumbled to fall.
During Christmas I'd be KrisKringle she'd be Mrs.Claus.
Together mentally we'd embark, and roam halls, conquering flaws.
A free flow of love with no stall.

After all she'd been there when I had no financial cause,
from others no love at all.

After all she'd been there through it all.

50. RACISM

It does exist,
seeing the darkness of our skins,
cops murdering innocent negro kids,
caught on tape, get suspended and do it again with no end.

Can't held those accountable of what ancestors did,
but we must remember that they're descendants
great, great, great grandkids;
and times change but the evil rely in the hearts of men.
How many times you see a cop brutality
of those of us with darkskin.

No jobs but penitentiary filled with darkskin men;
hundreds years ago slavery begin in reality it never end.

They took away water hoses and dogs
replaced them with mase and
tazors in hand.
Let us blossom and became financial
stable in their land, so they can
be in pockets with hands.

Racism within.....I will never end.

51. SYMBOLS ACHIEVED

From and through her a symbol of the
greatness of love was achieved.
I hope she would never leave.
She was one of the last of a dying breed.
From lunicy she was freed.
To posterity she held thr keys.
A way for me to be.

Her actions spoke louder then her words to me,
her symbol of greatness was achieved.

52. SEASONS CHANGED

Seasons changed.
Some people, places, and things got rearranged.
The concept and lit of 22-12, and 7-4 remained the same;
although now of days everybody doing their own things.
No loyalty, it's about what they can gain.
Fortune, more than fame.
Behind close doors doing any, and everything.
It's only a few things that remained the same,
everything else throughout the seasons changed.

53. DIVINE

She made me feel so divine.
She was bilingual, spoke English and Arabic,
and exercised the power of her mind.
She was just like me didn't use drugs, or alcohol,
or smoked cigarettes,
under no circumstances would she ever eat Swine.
Her and I together had our own ways to ease each others minds.
Live constructively throughout our life's time.
A cute one just so fine.
Could talk to her about anything, any time.
Wasn't interested in my money had her own grind.
She said to me," I love you all the time."
I'm glad you are mine, thanks for making me feel divine.

54. EVERY WAY

Soaked up things.
Was able to adopt to people, places, domestic and foreign things.
what sometimes others thought was scene.
Knew of the good, the bad, the ugliest, and evilist things.
A dream chasing fiend.
To others my love, life, of loyalty didn't mean a thing.
A indifferent some good, and bad changed.
Seeking something more than mere dollars or small change.
Remained the same in a bossful way of
thinking, doing, conquering,
conquered things.
To me loyalty, money, and power is and was everything.

Poets, and writers step away and let this king of kings have it's
shine, and way, and let my love,
dedication, and ability to write shine, shine
in each and everyway, everyday
in the most beautifulist way

55. READER

Advocate reader.
A child breeder.
A hunger feeder.
Such a great teacher;
had me thinking, contemplating much deeper.
Loved all God's creatures.
Stayed in religious books, and pamplets reading.
Felt life was meaningful through every episode,
and features.
A great woman, teacher, and advocate reader.

56. SOME UNDERSTANDING

Searching for some understanding.
Reverse and reprimand.
Some understanding.
Imperfect born in the flesh of a human as a man.
Confidence always thinking and saying, "yes I can."
Understanding others conditions and circumstances.
Knowledge to seek, and find some undersatnding.

57. ONCE AGAIN

Once again militia troops in form of men I assumed
was an ally, my friend, proved to be an enemy of the
state again, don't trust men.

Once again I listen to Satan allowed him to be my evil,
evilest twin, deceived my own self again.

Once again I thought she was genuine,
starting asking for money, inside my pockets she wanted in.

Once again theirs no end to the evil within
the hearts of women and men.

58. WRITE ABOUT

I write about the way I feel inside.
The first time I cried is when her,
she my grandmother died.
And then I started to pay more attention to sickness,
disease, poverty lives, red and itchy and drying my teary eyes.
Why did the young get killed, the good ones always die.
Some hurt feelings telling the truth instead of a lie.
DCFS babies real moms, and dads never hear them cry.
Let saints not court witnesses testify.
Let genuine love be showed for no reasoning
why for most that's a lie.

I write about the way I feel inside for our sins he died;
through me he's still alive.
A new way to be full of dignified pride.
And I love to write about even the good, and the bad side,
and the wonderful way the creator makes me feel inside.

59. THINGS BECAME

It's sad and strange how things became.
Those I love and trusted was the ones that was
no good for me similar to an addiction of cocaine.
The ones I did dirt with showed and told everything,
overtime was the ones on the stand pointed the finger and
blame.
My safe house was no secret thing, until it got buglarized witnesses
conveyed you, and your cousins name.

It's strange how things became he started back getting high,
a dopefiend.
Friends changed, don't remember the love I'd bring.
Those that was broke know have everything.

It's strange how things changed, how they became.
Things became, nothing or no one remained the same;
it's strange how people, places, and things became.

60. Institutionalize

An institution of lies;
from past times still crying over love ones demise.
Constantly putting forth an effort trying.
In a room of perforated doors,
locked behind, left behind.
A insane in mind.
Institutionalize stuck in time.

61. WORSE OR BETTER

For better or worse I'll choose you first,
until death drives me away in a hearse.
No sins for seeds to be curse.
A love the was willingly worth.
Maybe someday we'll make kids for you to give birth.
Who knows maybe we will be happily married until natural
cause of old age cremates us or puts us under the dirt.....
For you I love for better or worse.

62. HOME ALONE

I'm a big boy now I'm grown.
No more of the streets I shall roam.
I'm focusing on reality, what's going on.
In loving memories live on.
Home alone last past events, trigger my future rights
from wrongs.
Studying the biblical signs that never was gone today
they still live on.
Doing what i think is firm like stone,
making hardwork, and dedication be
futuristic prosperous in a zone.

Home alone I focus, study and work on the prosperity that is and
could be going on.....

Home alone.

63. OH WELL

Oh well it's my real story, and I shall tell it well.
Constant gun battles, and drug sells.
They already knew they going to hell.
Failures that in and out of jail,
each time keep trying to do it big on drug sells.

Oh well contaminated wake patients walk around by themselves
transalation needed to understand the slur of words exhaled.

Oh well I pray for those that's stuck in jails,
Heavenly Father please grant their appeals.

Oh well my destiny is to write, write music,
poetry, screenplays, and urban novels, realistic stories
for the audience to feel.

Oh well one day it's the ending of my story to tell,
as I rest in peace in a coffin, Heaven or Hell.....

Oh well.

64. GRANTED LOVE

A wish that was granted.
A love that was founded as soon as it landed.
A reason, define meaning of passion,
understanding.
A love that was uncanned.
Made me feel more than a man.
A grand stand.
A love that was granted, a love that was grand.

65. DELETED SCENES

Disease infected porn king and queens.
Life as it seems was the reality of shattered dreams.
In seven and eight grade, strung out, young dopefiends.
Back in the day pimps had women doing everything for
dollars signs of green.
Showed on the movie screen, but it was some deleted scenes.
Deleted scenes on how they slayed our civil rights kings.
As politicians sold dreams.
As our youth are lost floating down streams.
Life as it seems showed on certain parts,
the rest is deleted scenes.

66. DOWN ON MY KNEES

On the radio I begin to listen to this song that says I get down
on one knees.
It immediately got my attention for my
sick pornographic mind to be pleased.

But the song I get down on my knees was to pray,
to pray to God for the blessing, and impending heeds.
Through his love and mercy ones could definitely achieve.
Experiences don't overlook take heed.
Let his word be like nourishment for the
mind body, and soul, to feed.

The song meant that people must get down
on their knees to pray to breathe,
to live, to achieve.

down on ones knees.

67. YOUNG

Mother's crying for sons appeals to get won.
The devil keep imitating friendship running
around with his magical wand.
Some are dumb as they come,
no future plans to run, no where to go,
acting like they forgot where they come from.
Some loving the sounds of fire from a gun.
Young teenage ladies just want to come for the fun.
Young, and dumb, sprung like Donkey Kong.
No plans for the future to come.
Young and confused as they come.

68. HOW

How to sing.
How to live like a king or a queen.
A famous human being.
How to stand up without the chance to fall or lean.
How to bring miracles and the best out of even the worsest things.
How to live like an ancient emperor that orchestrated things.....

How, how to sing.

69. TEACH ME

Teach Me.
Teach me how, how to love.
Genuinely and pure as those angels up above.

Teach Me.
Teach me how to love,
be faithful as can be.
Endure the essence of opposed gender terrificly free.
And love whom that special someone is to be.

Teach me how love life, and the gift and powers that was giving
as a blessing unto me.

Teach Me.

70. REAL

At times reality

71. TIMELESS WOMBS

They say that time heals all wombs.
Well it's as I'm stuck in time, and there were no healing of wombs.
My destiny was buried alive in a temple of doom.
Sunny days of gloom.
In real life, lost, there was no wizard of oz
that would get me home soon.
Constant noises of humanized werewolves howling at fullmoons.
Blacks being called the N word or a coon.
No interest or concern about whom.
Peeping outta project windows no silver spoon.
Lady liberty was a lesbian that played with toys as tools.
Being fooled like fool.
I know I should forgive but I never forgave
or forgot when you wasn't there
when I needed you.

In reality time never healed all wombs it
just made me remember the times
when I was down and out when it seemed as if I was doomed.

72. TRUTH HURTS

She'd mention to me what I already knew that the truth hurts.
And she loved doing it when it hurts.
She said, I was the one that kept cheating,
she was faithful never winked her eye, had strange conversations,
or even flirt.
That humans are filled with deceit no interest in others
unless they could benefit,
use for what they was worth.
That it seemed as she loved me since birth,
but couldn't continue to be with me in conditions that wasn't
pure, that of dirt.

She said through me she learned a lesson,
love all but trust none for what it was worth.
Upon her departure I never seen her in many years
but heard she went celibate and had became
an evangelist at a baptist church;
at the end of each sunday she'd preach to the congregation
how evil Lucifer works, and how the truth surely hurts.

73. LOVE LIVED

Love lived in her heart and mind.
To her each day was Sweetish Day, and Valentine's.
When she'd see me, she'd jump into my arms hugging,
and kissing, loving me, and my kind.
She'd share her knowledge a gift to plant
seeds of growth for my mind.

Love lived in her heart and mind.
The sweetest and the best of any kind.
Loved being around me at all times.
My tree of life she love to ride, and climb;
as I arouse to the occasion that had to be erotic,
but yet divine.

Love lived in her heart, and mind,
and I pray that it'll never begin dying.

74. Life Flies

Life flies.
Watch and see how some get killed,
others naturally die.
The Devil has no demise.
Blinds that never did, and will see the sunrise;
they don't even want to have sight in eyes
to much death and destruction
and sickning ties that could be seen if sight was alive.

Life flies.
Juvenilles that's sentence to natural lives
for murdering, but only accessory to crimes,
didn't even know the laws within guidelines.
A life was wasted left in bars behind.
Shall be lost in the systematic system of times.

Life flies.
Those that reminsce of when they was little kids for candy
crying, to adolescents, to adults.
In time aged to see their own kids and grandkids crying.

Life flies.
Those that went to college for six or eight years
straight within time.
In the beginning knew success wouldn't
be denied but the long road
ahead seems as if it'll be forever, a long time.
The ride was finally over now it's a pleasurable grind.

Life flies.

75. BROWN BAG

As you open this brown bag that be that of a dime.
Let it stimulate your mind as cigars and lighters combine.
Let it be the best sensation known to mankind.
As clouds of smoke be that of symbolic signs.
Through this brown bag dime peace will
be multiplied as pregnancy's
will intertwine.
Within this brown bag dime the pleasure
will only last for a short period
of time, unless your finance is enclined.
Once you open this brown bag dime you
shall find the love that's enshrine,
as you in, and exhale moments at a time.

76. LIVE LIVING

It's life so you gotta live it.
Without suicide intentions.
Free from a prism of prison.
Doing less talking and more listening.
Be more forgiving.
Get out accomplish goals as conquered missions.
Yet and still it's your life live it,
but live it with the best wishes of great aspects,
and intentions.

77. POISION

Poision the community.
When it first started it was all about black power,
unity, and uplifting the black community.
Until those that was corrupt brought forth lunacy.
Taking the goverment funds and flooding dope, and guns
in the community.
More dope money divided us in our own communities.
There will never be no hope within opportunity for unity.
Death and destruction what I see daily, no immunity.
Days will continue to be gloomy.
Modern day slave ship, are overpacked
buses take inmates to prisons
as a tour duty.
Astray minds, dope, guns, and money poision our communities.

78. UTILIZED

She utilized foolish pride.
Made grown men cry.
On the stand they'd testify,
saying she was with them as an alibe.
She even used men from Great Britian, and Russia as spies.
Gas chambers and electric chairs for her they'd die.

She utilized her body to make religious men feel baptized,
love they realized,
the sleepwalkers she opened eyes,
help them get through troublesome times.
She should've been from Scandanavia as she scandolize.
Capotilzed.
Mastermind.
A massacre like St. Valentines,
as she utilize what she had to control minds.

She utilized her body and mind to make them feel divine.

79. DOING TIME

Needing restoration of good time, reciting the
Fataha and Holy Divine combine.
Secretly listening to those that's lying.
Watching time slowly go by doing time.
Wondering what's going on,
on the outside why did she leave me behind.
Nicotine used to ease minds.
Stripped of my youth and prime doing time.

80. A SLOW FORM OF SUICIDE

Because of her drinking she shall die.
Kids and grandkids shall cry.
She knew ahead of time it will be her time to die.
But she continue to bless the bottle while turning it up to the sky.
She told everyone she was in the best of health,
which was lie.
She wasn't scard to die.
Just wanted to drink liquor to ease her mind,
breeze through troublesome times.
In the bottle love she'd find.
Slowly drinking her life away as a slow form of suicide.
Died with a acholic beverage by her side.....
Suicide.

81. GAVE

Gave me something I could feel a love
that was real.
Stood by my side while I awaited on appeals.
Been there during my wersome ordeals.
Leader of the Navy Seals.
Religious but for me she'd kill.
So real I gave her my authentic golden seal.

She gave me something I could feel,
a loving that was real.

82. Lonely Days, and Nights

I never will forget those lonely dark nights,
sharpening up knives.
Wondering what might, as the state's attorney,
and my public defender verbally fight.
Literature being flown upon kites,
S.O.S. for more knives.
Crying out for someone to write.
Look what it came to this is my life.
I crapped out on the dice.
If I ever get free I wont be coming back twice,
no lonely days, and dark nights.

83. IMPERFECT SURFACES

Within this imperfect surfaces.
Stage fright of being nervous.
Imperfect surfaces that clearly show those whom are worthless.
The creator made us all imperfect.
As some misuse people for what they worth.
Lusting to see what's under a skirt.
Preachers that use profanity, and curse.
Truth that hurts, and dope fiends that's law clerks,
and bad nurse.....
Imperfect Surfaces.

84. This Horrible Word Titled Reality

This Satanic word titled reality caused
casualties, fatalities.
This word deplict no harmony, bad things to be.
Reality as kids dying in the street.
People never awakening from their sleep.
Reality should be deceased,
but it's a part of me.
Wars in the Middle East, no peace.
Housewives that cheat,
Ministers that aren't truly.
Things being what they seem.
Reality is the truth, not a sleeping dream.

85. TIME PREVAILED

Those that didn't raise hell serve their lives well,
shall prevail.
Shall receive granted wishes from wishing wells,
wishing love ones well.
The smart stayed back observed things
but kept them to themselves.
Soaked up knowledge, some would tell,
some they kept to themselves.
Found out that the pen was mightier than the sword,
and the truth in time could tell.
Dusted themselves off and tried it again, again after they failed.
Right now books are in libraries, in
bookstores, and on-line for sale.
Stayed focus, stayed smart to himself, became
a success story as time prevailed.

86. CONTINIOUS BLESSED

I hope that you'll continue to be blessed,
and that cast guardian angels with guard your flesh
until you're laid to rest.
Loving you has always been at it's all time high,
at it's best.
A 365 days of humanly fest.
A true love, I was blessed.
I hope, and pray that you'll continue to be blessed;
live a life with less stress, and paradise in the afterlife
will come a long time from now but it will be next.
God Bless.

87. Ms. Alphabet

A was for the love you always gave to me.
B was for the way you set my mind, and
heart free, thanks for loving me.
C was for pleasure of erotica, you pleasured me, in the bedroom
allowed my wildside to be free.
D was for the loyalty for me you let the public see.
E was for everything you did for me an
everlasting love that was static free.

88. TRIPS

Trips of guilt.
Dirty minds of filth.
Loose lips that shouldv'e been around to
sank slave ships before the slaves
entered or even appeared.
The book of Revelation is increasing more and more each year,
the mark of the beast is up and running it already been here.
The ones that's paid to serve and protect
is the ones black people fear.
Bless to still be living each day, week, month, and new year.
Taking memorable trips while I'm still here.

89. HISTORY REPEATS

In a day and age where dungeons of dragons was slayed.
Grown men slept in caves.
The slaying of gays.
No happy holidays.
Man made bombs that took lives away.
Time repeated itself to today.
The men in blue uniforms use tazors, guns, and pepper spray,
falsely acusing, and taking lives away.
Racism shown clear as day, and they still get away.
In ancient Africa blacks would kidnapp other blacks,
and take them to the ships to be slaves.
Today blacks work with the judge, and the state to place
other blacks in prison, as modern day slaves.
Whistle or compliment a white woman in segregation you shall
forever stay.
In reality history does repeats itself but only in a slightly
different way.

90. REALITY OF A DREAM

Is this reality of a mere dream I gave
myself a crown on my book Thug Poetry,
and made myself royal like a king.

Is it reality or a dream those that's
deceased I'll see them again once I
rest in peace and my soul is cast
to paradises Heavenly spring.

Is this reality or a dream all of those I
know and love will be set free from prison again
to be prosperous, uplifting, in the likeness of
God to roam the Earth like kings, and queens
as we did in Africa before Lucifer came.

Is it reality or a dream that I shall reign supreme,
live like a giant, step on conquering everything scene;
keep my mind and body clean.
Preach to those about the wonderful joy of what life brings,
like a prophet sent by the king of kings,
and live out my dreams.

91. CONSEQUENCES

Consequences that never came with
defense systems, no mechanism.
It was all about making wise or bad decisions.
Some wish they would've listen, before
they let the Devil trick them.
Lucifer uses all type of system from money
to adreline rush of violence in
in which he sicks you on them, go get him.
At younger ages had minds not on the
future of a productive system,
now the old ones sitting back with bank accounts in non-existence,
check to check living suffering from bad decisions, consequences;
which route should I take that one or this one.

92. LIFE OF MINES

Wish we could live life without ever dying.
Doing it over again making better decisions, turning back the
hands of times.
No rainy days only those filled with sunshine in this life of mines.
No shedded tears no such thing as crying.
Each day a happy birthday each night lovers
together as Happy Valentines.
Majority of the time everything is good and fine,
but only within this life of mines inside my own mind.

93. LOVERS AND FRIENDS

Intimate friends, a romantic blend.
God forgive for the bedroom we commit nasty sins.
I adored my woman, she worshipped her man.
Each time we hugged, and kiss she wanted
to do it again, and again.
We share a designated place, of intimate land.
She felt I was unhumane more than an average man;
I felt is if she was a gift, a starlight a gem.
Together skinny dips of swims.
Shared dreams of being celebrities with fans.
We both pushed each other to be more than
the average woman, and man.
I loved my woman, and she loved her man.

94. LADY PEACE

She said she wanted get more experience
in life, travel the sights to see.
She was against warfare, she wanted to increase the peace.
She went to homeless shelter, and roamed
the streets and fed those with
hunger pains something eat, plentiful like a daily fest.
She cried out to the Jehovah that poverty would cease.
She love people for who they be genuinely.
They'd ask why she'd do these things for free,
she said this is the way the creator made her to be.....
Lovely lady of peace.

95. Names In Vains

In name they used names,
and then that's when all the gun-fire, torches, gasoline,
and firely flames came.
People got hurt real bad,
but on flip alot knowledge was obtained;
be careful who you keep in your circle,
honor thy names, keep your mouth shut,
and stop it with the games.
It showed who was all grown up ready for battling,
it seperated the boys from man.
Trouble never went away after it came from using names in vain.

96. CIVILATION DYING

I've heard and seen with my own eyes that civilation is dying.
Law officials themselves steady committing crimes.
Baby having babies and the babies are being
beheaded, and shot by bullets at times.
Back to back funerals and I can't stop crying,
lost souls internally dying.
The blind leading themselves to dark roads as killers in mask
surround them from the front and behind
set themselves up for their own
demise.
Satan the dragon of the beast came with no surprise, no disguise,
it was time to go bye, bye, to meet his
eternal lake of fire and desire,
legacy of an empire.
No more drugs that can, and will take you higher.
No more pornographic desires.
Civilation coming to an end with no retire.

97. I COME AS I AM

Changing of circumstances.
I am as I come, I come as I am.
Before you I stand a strong independent man.
I can acheive greatness within this land.
To Satan the Dragon of the beast I throw down
my left hand.
Sacrificing for others all that can.
Executing plans.
Those that love me, and stuck by my side
together we stand.
Fathers should always be their for the kids,
if not you're less than a man.....
I am as I come, I come as I am.

98. Broken Homes

We came from broken homes.
Dad stayed locked up never really heard from him,
blocks on phones.
Mom stop selling the food stamps,
my stomach steady growling,
pretty much got a mind of his own.
Stamps for cash to the dealers now the cash is gone.
Mom would take a hit off the missle get geeked up in zone.
Child molesting uncles leave my little sisters alone.
Never had to go home when the street lights came on,
I wonder if mom even knew when I was
at home or when I was gone.
When I did go in no electricity candles lit up our project home.
Only in the sixth grade had to survive like I was grown.
Left for the city streets to roam.
The ViceLords, Disciples, and GangsterStones seen what I was on
all wanted to bless me in they wanted me to come on home.....
Broken Homes.

99. ADVICE

She'd always give good advice.
Told me to always think twice.
To others be twice as nice.
Always expressed how she felt which was right.
Kept things nice and tight.
Groovy and outta sight.
A bomb like dynamite.
And told me that after life those that
faithfully worship God shall reach paradise.

100. PROCESS

Process.
Process of constant regrets.
Cold and hot sweats.
Problems can't forget.
Living check to check.
Uncontrolling the destiny,
the kingdom be subside to sinful
Earthly flesh.
Constant deaths wondering whos next.
When will I cease to breathe my last breath.
A process of fast and slow mourning deaths.

UPCOMING URBAN NOVEL BY
ALAN HINES
KIDNAPPING

CHAPTER 1

I t was noon time scorching hot summer's day as the sunlight from the sky lit up the streets, the public was tired of blacks being murdered by the police, and a shame of how black on black crime continuous increase.

It was madness in the city streets two unarmed black males were killed by the punk police; one was home from college pulled over at a traffic stop the police shot and killed him in cold blood, the police lied and said that they thought his cell phone was a gun, the victim had no gun no prior arrest, no criminal background; the other black male that was shot was one of their very own, he was an off duty seargent, the white cops walked up to him to search him assuming he was a street thug, as the off duty seargent went to reach for his badge the racist cops shot him three times in the left side of his chest instantly seperating life from death as the four five bullets ripped through his heart he instantly fell to the concrete visualizing stars as he life no longer existed organs torn apart.

People of all colors came together on and every side of town; north, south, east, and even the west. Through the city streets they marched, and protest only in signs and symbols of peace. Hoping the violence would come to an end, that it would cease.

On Madison street people stood on all four corners as if they owned it. They were together as one, White, Blacks, Mexicans, Puerto Ricans, and even a few Arabics were presents; they all wore t-shirts that displayed Black Lives Matter, some were holding up signs that displayed honk you horn if you love Jesus.

Almost each car that rode past the crowds of people honked their horns; some yelled out there windows, "we love you Jesus," as others yelled out there windows loud and clear, "black lives matter."......

Daily around the city meetings were being held in churches, unioun halls, amongst various other places but all on one accord to stop the violence.

Hundreds of protestors peacefully marched up to city hall with picket signs, telling those at city hall that the violence just gotta stop......

The mayor of the city, and the police commisioner came together and made a statement on the news saying that he, and the Chicago police Department will be doing all they can to decrease the violence in the city streets......

Mysteriously three black teenage girls came up missing, and had been missing for many months; the authorities had no leds to there whereabouts......

After a innocent twelve year old black girl was killed by stray bullets, her mother was interviewed at the scene of the crime by the channel 9 news......

Running down her face drowning tears of sorrow knowing that her twelve year old daughter was dead wouldn't be here to live to see another day tomorrow.

She cried out on the channel 9 news in front of the camera for people stop the violence.

The grieving mother told the news," the police don't give a fuck about us, if they killing our young black males, what makes everybody think they give a fuck about finding those missing girls. It wouldn't surprise me if they never find the bitch that killed my little girl."

Oh how her angry harsh words was so true.

The authorities searched and searched, did a thorough investigation, but no killer was found and charged with the murder of twelve year old Shante Smith......

CHAPTER 2

"The niggas off the low-end been eating real good, them niggas been performing," Kuda said. "They been kidnapping niggas, they be trying to grab any nigga getting some real bread," Big Shorty said. "Awwww that's how them niggas been eating like that," Kuda said. "What they do is they kidnapp a nigga for a healthy ransom, or rob a nigga for some weight, and then whatever they get they invest it in buying more weight, flooding the low end with hella narcotics," Big Shorty said. "That's smart," Kuda said.....

Early one sunday morning Kuda sat in the park across the street, slightly up the block from where the shorties slang his rocks.

Big Shorty walked up to Kuda, as Kuda set fire to a Newport long, Kuda took a long pull off the square, as Big Shorty could see, and feel a sense of distress.....

"Man Big Shorty we got to hit us a lick, rob a nigga, kidnapp a nigga or something," Kuda said. "Your joint doing pretty good, why you wanna take some other nigga shit," Big Shorty said. "My joint only sell like a stack or two a day, it take me two or three days to scrap up the money to re-copp to go get another four and a baby, you feel me," Kuda said. "But you still eating alot of these niggas out here broke ass hell,"

Big Shorty said, "True, but look at the niggas off the low end they got joints selling 10 or 20 thousand a day, some of them even got two or three joints, selling weight and robbing niggas all at the same damn time, that's what I call getting money," Kuda said.....

Big Shorty remained silent for a brief moment knowing that Kuda was speaking the truth.....

"But Kuda it's so much chaotic madness, that comes along with sticking up. Them niggas off the low-end in constant danger," Big Shorty said. "I'm already in constant danger for all the shootings I've been doing over the years, representing the business for the hood, I deserve to be eating good, fuck the dumb shit I gotta hit me a lick," Kuda said.

Big Shorty remained silent again for a brief moment realizing the realization of what Kuda was talking about.....

Kuda joint started to get sweating more by the police because all ths shooting, that was going on in the area. It was hard for Kuda to work because of the police sweating his joint, and because the hood was in war. Now Kuda really knew he had to hit a lick to get some fast cash.....

More and more Kuda talked to Big shorty about hitting a lick.....

Kuda and Big Shorty ended up getting up with a few guys from the hood that was highly interested in kicking in some doors, and taking another nigga shit.....

A few guys from the hood knew of a few houses on the other side of town where niggas was holding drugs and money at.

Kuda, Big Shorty, and the few guys from the hood kicked in a few doors hitting licks. Each lick they came up on several thousands outta each house, which wasn't shit to them because they had to split it five ways each time.

Kuda was hungry to eat, he was tired of small time nickels and dimes he wanted to do it big.....

One of the guys from the hood that they went on the licks with seen how well Kuda, and Big Shorty performed when they ran in them houses, and decided to set them up to kidnapp his sister boyfriend. The guy couldn't do it himself because his sister boyfriend knew him, and he didn't want to send nobody else but Kuda, and Big shorty because other people was messy and would fuck shit up.

The guy sister would be the one to set her boyfriend up, she was tired of the nigga he was to cheap, but the nigga had long money.....

They planned on kodnapping him for thirty thousand, splitting it up evenly four ways a piece, therefore each individual would get seventy-five hundred a piece.....

Kuda was charged up, this is the kind of lick he was interested in hitting.....

Two in the morning as the streets lights lit up the sky, Kuda and Big Shorty set in the car parked several cars behind their soon to be victims car.

Kuda took a long hard pull of the last of his Newport long, inhaling, and exhaling the smoke out of his nose as if it was a blunt filled with loud.

Once Kuda was finish smoking the cigarette he threw the butt out the window.....

Outta nowhere comes this guy sister, and her boyfriend out the door walking down the porch.....

Her and her boyfriend made their way to the back of his car, and started tongue kissing him in which seemed so delghtful for the both of them.

As their lips and tongues disconnected he opened his trunk searching for a purse he had bought her.....

As he lift his head up trying to give her, her bag outta nowhere Kuda appeared instantly back hand slapping the shit out of him upping a big ass gun putting it to his stomach. As Big Shorty came from the back putting a gun to his head forcing him inside the trunk, as the girlfriend cried tears pleading with them to stop; she put on a great performance, she should've won a Oscar for.

As the trunk closed she started smiling, glad that they got his ass. But she continued crying and pleading with them to stop just in a case a neighborhood was watching.

Kuda drove the victim off in his own car as Big shorty followed Kuda in his car; the girlfriend ranned in the house crying as they pulled off.

Once she made it in the house she called her brother and told him," they got his bitch ass".....

She left out the house went to her car and drove slowly to the nearest police station which took her approximately twenty minutes.....

She ran inside the police station crying emotional tears, that seemed really, real.

She told the police that her boyfriend was kidnapped, she gave up false identities of the kidnappers.

The police asked why didn't she call immediately after it happen. She told the police that the kidnappers robbed her for her phone and money so she couldn't call, and that she went to two of the neighbors house and they never answered their door bells.....

After finishing the police report she went home sipped some wine, relaxed in a hot bubble bath, thinking of the things she'd do with her seventy five hundred once she had it in her possession.....

Two days passed overlapsing into nights; now it was crunch time. Kuda and Big Shorty had made arrangements for the kidnapped victims people to run thirty stacks,

They was supposed to leave the money in a trunk of a car parked near a shopping center that was closed, it was closed because it was the middle of the night, but during the day it would regularly be open.

Before they even made it there with the thirty stacks Kuda, and Big Shorty circled all around the area, there were no police cars or unmarked cars nowhere to be found.

Right before the victims people brought the money, Kuda and Big Shorty watched from a far distance with binoculars as some old lady came, bent down got the keys from under the left back tire as instructed.

As she opened the trunk Kuda, and Big shorty begin cheering, giving each other constant high fives.

She put the money in the trunk and the keys back under the left tire as instructed, and walked away disappearing into the night.

Kuda and Big shorty waited for approximately twenty minutes just to make sure the coast was clear, then they text the chick they had designated to go pick the money up.

She made it there in no time. As she walked up to the car bent down picked up the keys from under the left tire, opened up the passenger door.

As soon as she sat down, before she could even close the door, twenty unmarked cars surrounded her out of nowhere, all she heard was sirens and seen guns upped on her from every which way. It was impossible for her to get away.....

The police grabbed her by the neck slamming her face to the concrete, cuffed her up, roughed her up a little and put her in the back of one of the police cars.

The police drove her, and the vehicle that the money was in to the police station to further pursue their investigation.....

Kuda, and Big Shorty watched the whole thing their binoculars, shook the fuck up.....

Once the police left Kuda, and Big shorty pulled off confused not knowing what to do.....

Shortly after leaving the seen of the crime Kuda stopped at a nearby pond and threw his cell phone in it. From Big Shorties phone he called his phone carriers hot line, telling them his phone was stoling and had been missing for hours, he had insurance, so they'd definitely replace it. He threw his phone in the pond, because he text the chick that the police just grabbed from his phone, so if the police went through her phone and linked the text back to his phone he could say it wasn't him, that someone stole his phone.....

As they proceeded back driving home they both was worried, wondering if the girl would play fair ball, or switch up like a bitch and snitch.

Kuda was driving as Big Shorty kept looking back every two or three minutes to see if they was being followed by the cops.

"What the fuck, why is you steady looking back for," Kuda asked? "The police might be following us," Big Shorty said. "The police is not following us if the police wanted us we'd already been got. I hope the bitch didn't tell, I know she did," Kuda said.

"Straight up," Big Shorty said.

Once they made it to the police station at first she played like she didn't speak any English.

She was Boricua, Kuda had nicknamed her the thrill seeking Puerto Rican, because she was adventurous loved violence. Even when the police grabbed her and roughed her up, she loved it.

Months prior to her arrest Kuda, and Big Shorty use to fuck her at the same time; she loved two dicks at once she preferred one in the mouth, and another in her pussy at the same time as Kuda, and Big Shorty would choke her and slap her around in the midst of sex.

She was a bad bitch she just got an adrenaline rush off hardcore shit.....

As the police proceeded questioning her even when they went to get her an interpreter she winded up speaking to them in English.

The cops came to find out her name was Maria Rodriguez. She had been to the joint before twice, once for a kidnapping, and the other time for robbery, and was still on parole for the robbery.

She lied and told the cops that someone paid her to go pick up that car, only because they was pulled over by the police for driving with no license, and once the police left they came back to leave an additonal set of keys under the left tire so she could pick the car up since she had license. To assure them that she had no knowledge of a kidnapping.....

The police knew her story was bullshit, so they asked her who didn't have license and sent her to pick the car up for that reason. She told them she couldn't give any names, because she didn't know what was going on.....

The police pleaded with her for hours to give up a name or names, she didn't tell them shit.

They ended up fingerprinting her processing her in and charging her with kidnapping and sending her to the County Jail.

Of course she didn't want to be locked up, but she wasn't worried at all, on her bus ride to the County she'd vision all the pussy she'd be eating once she made it within and started mingling and getting to know the other girls.

After a few days rolled around Kuda, and Big Shorty didn't know what to do with the victim. Normally in a situation like that the individual that had been kidnapped would be put to death since the people got the police involved.

Kuda, and Big Shorty contemplated long and hard about killing the Vic, but decided not to, because if they did they could possibly give Maria a conspiracy to murder, and she could start singing the blues to the police telling them everything.....

After about a week in the middle of the night they dropped the vic off and left him in a abandon building still blindfold and tied up, called his people and the police and told them where to get him from.

Kuda and big Shorty wasn't worried about the vic sicking the police on them; he didn't even never see their faces, they had on masks, and even if he did see their faces he didn't know them or there whereabouts because they were from different sides of town.....

After a few weeks Kuda, and Big Shorty was able to get in touch with Maria, she'd call them collect continously.

Come to find out, she was a down bitch, didn't tell the police shit; they kind of figured she didn't snitch because she knew where Kuda, and Big Shorty lived, and if she would've told the police would've been at their house by now.

Kuda and Big Shorty wanted to bond her out, or atleast put up something on her bond, but she couldn't bond out because she was on parole, she had a parole hold.

Kuda and Big Shorty started sending her money orders constantly to make sure she was straight in there.....

The vic they kidnapped continued dating, fucking around with the chick that set him up to get kidnapped, never in his wildest dreams would he even assume that she was the one that set him up to get kidnapped. Later in life he even ended up getting the bitch pregnant with twins.....

CHAPTER 3

B lack lives matter was getting to be an even more major issue. Peaceful protest even seemed to get violent. The black politicians and even black cops was sick and tired of being sick and tired of all the killing blood spilling of the black population.....

More and more teenage black girls would mysteriously come up missing. More and more gangs were waring harder throughout the city, North, South, East, West.....

The black people begin to have meetings quite often mainly at churches, and Union halls.....

One night they had a meeting to their surprise unnumbered white people, and Latinos showed up to support black lives matter; they wore shirts and buttons displaying all lives matter.

The meeting became slightly hostile as not the blacks or Latinos, the white people started snapping out saying that racism does exist, and they were tired of blacks losing their lives by gunfire, especially from white-police officers that gets paid from tax-payers money to serve and protect the community, when all along they were causing the deaths and destruction within the community, it so much killing and hate, seemed as if it was no-love, nor unity.....

They allowed this one white lady to approach the front to get on the stage onto the pulpit, to preach the bullshit.....

"If we study our past history blacks were hung, lynched by white mobs, shot down by angry white fire squads, and even killed by the police as they same way today. With the 1900's many white that committed hate crimes against blacks were either investigated by the police, some even were put on trial and as documenting they were liberated of their crimes. History does repeat itself in a way. Now technology is advance and I've seen with my own eyes on video, shown white police killing black men, and even after shown on video surveillance, the officer still gets acquitted of all charges someway somehow.

If a black man kills another black man he'll immediately be placed in prison until trial, and in large unnumbered cases he'll get found guilty. And if a black man kills a white person in most cases that black man will eventually get found guilty, and sentenced to excessive time in prison possibly until he dies of natural causes. That's one of the main problems with the police brutality and unjustified murders of blacks they know they can get away with it because they are the police. What need to happen is that the police need to start getting persecuted and sent to prison for their crimes of hate. Until they start getting convicted of the crimes the madness won't stop," she said.....

As she dropped the mic tears flowed freely from her eyes. Knowing that racism was still alive. Lucifer's legacy of racism and hate wasn't decreasing any, but instead it begin coinciding with his sick enterprise.

Everyone in the church begin clapping, and cheering impending her speech.....

This one lady sat in the back all the way in the corner dressed in black with a veil over her face as if she was going to a funeral; she cried silently of sorrow drowning watery tears that shall forever shed throughout her lifetime of years wishing it never happen, wishing her son was still living, still here.....A few years prior to that date her son was wrongfully shot down, murdered by the nation, better known as the police; the two officers that killed her son did stand trial, and was acquitted of all charges against them of her sons murder.....

Soon as the second individual stepped to the pulpit to voice his opinion, gun shots rang out, five of em, sounding like a canon was outside.....

Everyone in the church got frightened, and then within rage everyone ran out the church, not scared of the gun-fire, but pissed the fuck off.

They ran out the front door in a rage eagerly trying to see who was standing, and what for.....

As majority of the people had exited the church it was still more rushing out the front door, one woman spotted a guy up the block laid out on the sidewalk.

She yelled out to everyone, "it somebody down there laid out on the sidewalk."

Everybody rushed to the individual that was laid out.

Come to find out it was a teenage boy that was still breathing, living. He had been shot once in the ass, and once in both of his legs.....so that meeting was officially over for that night.

As they approached him they seen him shot up as blood ran perfusely down the sidewalk he'd repeatidely keep saying, "I can't believe that pussy ass nigga shot me;

I can't believe that pussy ass nigga shot me; I can't beleive that pussy ass nigga shot me," he said. "Who shot you son," one of the gentlemen in the crowd of church people ask? "I don't know who shot me," he said.

He was lying like a motherfucker, who knew exactly who shot him.

"They called the police already, they should be here soon, it's a police station nearby," the gentlemen said.

In no time flat the police arrived first, and the ambulance arrived shortly after.

The guy that had got shot told the police he didn't know who shot him, although he did. He didn't want the nigga that shot him to get locked up, he wanted to kill the bitch.....

Several days later the guy was let out of the hospital but had to be in a wheel-chair, not for a long-term, only to his ass, and legs were well.....

The same day he was let out of the hospital, the same night the guy that shot him was killed, somebody shot him with a double barrel shotgun taking half his face off.

As homicide started their investigation they called it the face off murder. They never found any witnesses or suspects, so no one was never convicted or even charged with that murder.....

It seemed as if day by day the city streets, begin to be filled with madness, killings, mournings, sirens, and sadness.

It was clicks within the same gangs waring against each other. Rivals was waring against each other even harder. You had certain gangs that was into it with two different gangs at once. Then it was certain gangs that was into it with their own gang and into it with the opps all at the same time.

Part of the reason why gangs was tearing it up with each other was because years prior, and even to the present date the feds was locking up all the heads of gangs; everytime a new head would step up and get in play the Feds would find a way to lock his ass up to, leaving no law and order within the streets amongst; just like a body once you cut the heads of the body will fall. It was uncontrollable anarchy within the city streets.

Throughout the city streets it was constant gun-fire, like it was New Years Eve.

Some of the rappers changed the nickname from The Windy City to The City of No Pity.

Shit got so fucked up they start killing niggas in broad daylight on purpose.....

On one side of town two gangs was waring so hard they just start shooting ata ny and everybody that was affiliated with the oppositions.

One time they caught one of the opps main-girl walking the dog; they shot her and the dog. She lived the dog died.

The same nigga that girl and dog they shot, in return he caught an opp grandma-ma walking home from church with her bible in hand. He walked up to her upped a black .44 automatic to her stomach. Her smile instantly turned into a frown as she said, "praise the lord son," whole heartidely.

As he walked in the alley by gun point she didn't say a word, she wasn't scared at all not one bit, she feared no man but God.

As he walked her to the middle of the alley he seen a car slow down by the alley, he thought it was a detective car; he made her get on her knees on the side of a garbage can, he stood on the side of the garbage can faking like he was pissing. He immediately notice that it wasn't the police.

He looked down at her, she was on her knees praying. She wasn't worried about herself, she was praying for him, praying to the Heavenly Father that he would forgive him for his sins, and that someday he'd convert his life over to the Lord.....

Three shots ripped through her head, leaving her for dead, more blood to shed.

After the third shot many people came out on their back porches, not witnessing the actual murder, but witnessing seeing him fleeing from the scene of the crime.....

What the killer didn't know was that she was more than happy to die or be killed, because she knew that upon death she'd finally meet the king of kings, the lord of lords, God, and his only begotten son Jesus Christ to have eternal peaceful life in Heavens paradise.....

The same day the opps found out who killed his grandmother, him and his guys tore the streets up. The niggas from the other side tore it up as well they went round for round.

It was like a riot in the hoods they were from. They burned down houses, and cars, niggas from each side got shot up bad or killed.

They even burn up some houses waited until the opps came running out and shot them up murdered they ass.....

A few days after grandma was murdered homicide apprehendid the killer taking him to jail charging him with that murder. What the killer didn't know was that is that many people witness/saw him running up the alley after he shot her, and that he'd never see the streets again, he'd spend the rest of his natural life rotting away in a jail cell.....

All the violence brought forth more police harrasement of blacks.....

More protesting about Black Lives Matter.

In various places on each side of town you'd see large numbers of people on corners, holding up signs saying honk your horn if you love Jesus, some of the people had on Black Lives Matter T-Shirts, as others had on All Lives Matter T-Shirts. Almost every car that road pass honked their horn, some hollered out "we love you Jesus, Black Lives Matter." A small percentage of passing cars parked their cars joining in on the peaceful protest.....

A few guys in the crowd dipped off to the alley, all you heard was 3 gunshots from a .45 sounded off as the crowds on the streets immediately dispursed. The guys in the alley ran back to the crowds blending in running away as if they didn't know where the shots were coming from, but simply trying to get away from the danger like everyone else. They did that because they joint was right up the street and they couldn't sell their dope with protesters on location, so that quick smart way to get rid of them.

As time progressed along more and more black girls were being kidnapped in various places around the United States; the situation begin to strike controversy, because all of them black.

In the past the black community slightly lost focus on the girls that were being kidnapped, because they found out that a hand full of the missing girls that they thought had been kidnapped, had ran away from home, for different reasons and stayed gone for long periods of time, but eventually returned on their own free will.....

CHAPTER 1

It was the middle of the night as the blue, and white police car drove swiftly up the block. The car slowed down as it reached the end of the block as the passenger examined the address of the house to make sure it was the correct address they were looking for.....

Inside the police car was two white police officer's.....

"Is the address 4955," the driver asked the passenger? "Yes it is," the passenger responded.....

The officer's parked their squad car and they bailed out of it swiftly. As they walked up the stairs before they even got a chance to ring the door bell five shots of gun fire rang out....

Two gun shots hit one of officer in the back of the head twice. The other three shots hit the other officer in the back of his head twice, and once in the neck.....

The got shots had came from across the street from the third floor of an abandon building.....

Within seconds Will, and Black was gathering up all their shit trying to swiftly exit the abandon building.....

"Hurry up," Will told Black. "Hold on I drop the banacolus," Black said.....

Once Black picked up the banacolus off the floor, they ran to the stairs, and start running down the stairs at top speed.....

They made it their car which was in front of the abandon building.....

Black made it to the drivers side of the door reached in his pocket, and couldn't find the cars keys, he panicked, and started searching all his pockets

"What the fuck unlock the door," Will told Black. "I can't find the keys," Black said, as he continued searching all his pockets, even the back pockets of his pants. "Look in your front pocket, the left one," Will said.

Black stuck his hand all the way in his left pocket and came up with the keys, unlocked the door got in the car reached over and unlocked the passenger side of the car. Started the car up, and got in it, and smashed off with the pedal to the metal, burning rubber.....

At top speed Black was putting forth his best effort to get away.....

"Slow down," Will said. "Slow down, we just killed two police officer's I'm trying to get away," Black said. "Man slow this car down," Will said in a demanding manner.....

Black started to slow down a little.....

"Man slow this car down, you gone get the police to start chasing us. When you do dirt like that you got to leave the scene at ease, that way the police don't get on to you. I'f they see you driving fast that automatically know what it is. Now if they see you driving regular with your seat belt on blending in with the hundreds of cars passing by they are less likely to try to get at you. Even if you drive right pass them after doing dirt, as long as you're driving regular nine times out of ten they aint gonna fuck with you, becuase they'll think you a regular car just driving past," Will said.....

Black slowed the car down driving at regular speed.....

They drove to a secret hide away only to stash the guns. Then they drove to another secret hide away where the usually have meetings.....

Once they made it there Will begin to think about what they just had did, and the mistakes they made.....

"You did a good job, but the way we did that was messy, we got to make it better next time. We can't slip up and drop things like we did the banacolus, and we definitely can't misplace car keys. You keep it in your mind exactly where the car keys are at. Just think if we wouldn't have found those keys we'd probably had to make it home on foot, chances are we would've been chased by the police or even caught. We would've looked real suspicious walking down the street dressed in all black carrying large equipment concealed in bags," Will said.....

"You know that no matter what happens whenever you do dirt like that you must not tell nobody not even those that's part of the Black National family," Will said.

Black remained quiet staying attentive listening to Will as Will would feed his brain powerful knowledge.....

Will, and Black were part of an organization called Black Nationals. Will was the founder of Black National, Black was the co-founder. Some may would've considered them a gang, but the Black Nationals considered themselves to be an organizations that was in existence for the upliftment of black people.

The Black Nationals was a small organiztion that consist approximately thirty members. Every once in a while they'd accept a new member. Only in meetings they'd wear all black. They did a little protesting, and preaching in schools, and churches. But mainly they focus on trying to get blacks education, on a higher level of higher learning so that blacks would be successful on a positive note. When they did their protesting, and preaching they didn't represent Black National, they represented for the black people. Black National was like a secret society.

The Black Nation was against crime, and any usage of drugs, alcohol, and tobacco usage. The only crimes that the Black nationals was up with was violent hate crimes against white people.....

The next day after they killed them two police Black Nationals held a meeting in one of the members basement that was made up like a church. Will led the meeting as usual.....

"It's about the growth, and developement of the black community. We are black, and beautiful, black beauty's. It's time for change, and improvement, and we must do what it takes to change, and improve. We were once kings, and queens we ruled the place we once lived in before the white devils came in. We governed, and control our own lands. Our women even walked around bare chested showing of their beautiful black breast not as a sex symbol to men, but as a way of being. The women did this until the white devil came along, and made it seem wrong. As we go back the Alpha in bible the snake Satan tricked Adam, and Eve into thinking nudity was an impurity, and abnormal the white devils did the same to us. Every black brother, and sister in the divine area right now hug one another, as a form of undying love unity for your black brothers, and sisters" Will said to the Black Nationals as they all stood at attention dressed in all black unlocking their hands from behind their backs to tightly hug one another listening vividly to Will as he continued to preach.....

Overtime the Black National's membership slightly grew, as the Black Nationals terror of vicious hate crimes dramatically increased.....

One late cold winter's night Ruby ran up to an parked squad car occupied by two white officer's with her coat open, and her shirt slighty torn with her big beautiful brown breast bouncing.....

"He tried to rape me, he tried to rape me," Ruby said to the officers.....

The officer was so mesmerized by the sight of those big ole titties, that they wasn't able to respond right back it was as they were in a trance.....

Within no time the officer's came back to reality.....

Both officer's got out of the car.....

"Who tried to rape you," one officer asked with his eyes on her breast. "Where he at," the other officer asked with his eyes stuck on her breast. "He in this alley," Ruby said.....

Ruby ran back to the alley as the police got in the squad car to follow her.

As they made it to the part of the alley were Ruby was at they wondered why she didn't get in the car with them instead of running back to the alley on her own.

They rushed out of their car before they could say a word Ruby sprayed them in the face with Mace. Then she begin cutting one in the face back to back, as he grabbed his gun busting shots unable to see due to the Mace in his eye he accidently shot his partner in the eye twice. The bullets went to his brain instantly leaving him for dead.

The Mace in the officer's eyes made him feel as if he was blind, as Ruby stabbed in his throat a few times he dropped his gun, as he himself collapsed to the ground Ruby got on top of him stabbing in both his eyes, his face, and his head, as he squealed like a pig, Ruby snatched his life away from him.....

After the short period of drama Ruby vanished away from the scene of the crime.....

Ruby was a member of the Black Nationals, she was thoroughbred, had more heart then most of the members in the Black Nationals, and she knew how to do her dirt smart, and kept her mouth shut.....

Days later Ruby walked up to some of the Black National members as they were discussing the two police getting killed. Never in their wildest dreams would they have imagined that Ruby was the one who killed the two police.....

Didn't nobody know what Ruby did, she had learned from Will to do dirt, and to keep your mouth close, that way you wouldn't have to worry about no one telling the police.....

Sometimes members of the Black Nationals would do dirt to white people by themselves, and keep their dirt to themselves; other times they'd get together in numbers to do dirt, they called it war games.....

One late quiet night Will, Black, Ruby, and two other members of Black National, Dennis, and Tody, all decided to play war games.

Sometimes they'd split up to play war games. This time they decided to do it together, but in two different cars that would be right behind one another.

They'd use the women as driver's so that way after they did their dirt the men could duck down in the cars as if the women were in the car driving by themselves; that way it would be less likely the police to bother a car only occupied by one woman.

Will, Black, and Ruby was in one car. Tody, and Dennis trailed behind them in their car.....

While driving on a quiet side street unexpectedly they spotted a black prostitute just finished performing hardcore erotica for a white trick in a white Sedan. Black whom was sitting in the back seat of the first car signaled Todie, and Dennis to pull over.

Both cars pulled over on the other side of the street a short distance from the white trick in the sedan, and cut their lights off swiftly. The prostitute exited the car, and walked swiftly anxious to spend her earned money on buying her some dope.

He was so mesmerized by the sexual experience he just had with the prostitute that he sat in the car smoking a cancer stick oblivious to his surroundings and what was soon to come.....

Outta nowhere three shots sounded off like canons, "dooock, dooock, dooock." One bullet hit the white trick in the bottom part of the back of his head the other two hit him in his back.

Will felt wonderful after he shot the man up three times, as he ran back to the car the sounds of victorious trumpets sounded off in his head.....

As Will made it to the car all three men in both cars duck down, as the ladies smoothly coasted off as if nothing never happen the way Will taught them how to do it.....

"Did you get him, did you kill him," Ruby asked excitedly? Will begin slightly laughing. "I don't know I hope so," Will said.

About an hour later they found another victim. A white guy dressed up in a three piece suit walking down the street as if he owned the street with a briefcase in his hand.....

They pulled both cars around the corner Will got out and walked up to the man. As Will approached him the white gentleman looked up at Will with a smile upon his face on verge of greeting him. Will upped on him hitting him three times in the forehead the bullets ripped through his skull pushing half of his head off. The sight off it made Will so happy.

Will ran back to the cars jumping for joy.....

What Will didn't know was that the man he had killed was a homicide detective whom was coming home from work. Thw detective decided to walk home from work instead of driving, because his head was clouded by the constant murders, and secretive racism that was going on in his precinct, and around the world in general. The detective was on his way home to be with his black wife, and his two bi-racial kids.....

Later that night both car loads were mad, and jealous that Will had did all the killings himself that night. It was almost daybreak, and they had decided to call it a night. Ruby spotted this older white guy standing a bus stop on a main street.

She pleaded with Will to let her kill him. Will told her no the women were only used in war games to assist the men to get away. Ruby debated with Will that men, and women should be as equals especially the black men, and women. Although Ruby, and Will only debated for a short period of time Will decided to let her free to commit murder.

Both cars pulled around the corner, and parked, Will reloaded the gun handt Ruby the gun, and told her to be careful. Once Ruby got out of the car Tody, and Dennis looked at her stun with no clue of what was going on.

As Ruby started to walk to her destination Will got out the car, and told Tody, and Dennis that Ruby was getting to kill the white chump at the bus stop.....

As soon as Will got back in his car, and slammed the door he heard six shots go off. The shots was so loud that it was if the were coming from only a few feet from him.....

Ruby had walked up to the white guy on the bus stop, and asked for a cigarette the white guy made a racial slur, as Ruby upped on him shot him up six times unloading her .38 revolver as the bullets ripped through his flesh she knew he wouldn't live through tips of hallows to see a better day tomorrow.....

In no time Ruby made her way back to the car got in the driver's side, and smoothly coasted off.....

As they drove away to their secret hide away they all visioned Ruby taking away that white chumps life.....

Right then, and there Will knew Ruby was a winner, and a proud member of Black National's.....

Overtime Will wondered, and wondered how would it be possible for his dream of Black Nationlism to come to reality. He wondered how would blacks begin to govern politics in their own communities, how would blacks become more book smart through education, and how would their be more blacks becomming business owners.....

Will, Black, amongst others in the Black National worked for the white men. And those that didn't work for the white men were either mechanics or beauticians whom didn't have their own shops yet. But all of the Black Nationals had one thing in common they all long for the day to come were they all lived like kings, and queens on earth legitimately without any crimimal grinding.....

"Black beauty's I'd like to thank each, and every one of you for showing up today it's my privilege to be part of this organization.

Since we first started it's been all talk, and not enough action. We gotta figure out a way for improvement," Will said as everyone started to clapping, and cheering.....

Everyone started clapping and cheering because they'd been feeling the same way.....

Within the next meeting Will had came up with a plan to make black people slightly advance. He told them that were mechanics, and beautician to train other blacks those trades; not just the blacks in Black National, but black people in general. Will told them to do that so that they would be able to make extra money outside of their day jobs, and eventually be able to take their trade and earn money, and be able to open up small shops. Will also told the Black Nationals to go to libraries, and attend college to study politics, that way they'd be able to slightly advance on a political level. The Black Nationals followed instructions.....

Within only weeks Will would talk to members of Black National, and he could tell by their conversations that they'd followed orders. Will felt good that he planted mental seeds of growth that was slowly starting to grow.....

Over time the Black Nationals continued to play war games. The war games had slowed down dramatically, most of Black National was more interested in the knowledge of being book smart.....

Ruby, and Will feel in love with war games, most of the time when they played them it would be just them two.....

One night after playing war games Will, and Ruby decided to go over his house to spend a night simply because it was late, and both of them were to sleepy to drive far. Will lived closer to where they was at than Ruby did so that's why they decided to go to his house. It was cool because Ruby's husband was a part of Black National, and Will girlfriend whom didn't live with him was real cool with Ruby, and her husband.....

Once they almost made it to Will's house it started to rain. When they made to Will's place they couldn't find a park therefore they had to park all the way up the street, and get out and run to his house in the rain in which left they clothes all wet up.....

"You can go in my bedroom, and look in the closet my girlfriend left some clothes of hers in there, you can get a pair of her clothes, get in the shower, and change clothes. You can sleep in my bedroom I'll just sleep on the couch," Will said.....

Will sat the couch feeling uncomfortable because of the wet clothes, and because he was fighting his sleep he wanted to wait until Ruby was done so he could get in the shower.....

Within a few minutes Ruby came out the bathroom ass hole naked with only a towel drying off her hair.

Will stood to attention looking at Ruby as if he'd just seen a ghost.....

"Ruby what are you doing," Will asked? "I'm drying my hair," she said calmly, and innocently. "Ruby where your clothes at," Will asked? "They're in the bathroom. I remembered what you had said at a meeting one time that we were free to walk around naked in Africa before the white man came, and poisioned our minds," Ruby said.

Their stood this naked beautiful black young lady. She stood five feet, chocolate super thick with such a cute face, and naturally curly hair.....

This girl on some bullshit, she know she married to one of our black brothers, and she want to put me in this situation, Will thought to himself.....

She stopped drying her hair off dropped the towel on the floor and walked up to Will, and gently hugged him around his waist, as he didn't attempt to reject. She looked him in his eyes and told him," I love you." "But you're married," he said. "But I'm only human, and I love you, and I want you take me as your queen, and do whatever you want to me, I belong to you," she said.

Will begin smiling, and laughing right before their lips connected, as they began playing the French kissing game that seemed like forever.....

Eventually Ruby snatched her lips away from his and fell to her knees. She looked up at him, and asked him, "can I suck your dick." "Go ahead," he said.

Ruby eagerly broke the button off his pants, and then unzipped them.

Once she pulled his dick out of his underwear she paused speechless she couldn't believe how long, and fat his dick was, she had never seen or had a dick that big.....

She wrapped her left hand around the back of the dick, then she tried putting it in her mouth she almost couldn't open her mouth wide enough to put it in but she finally did.

She stroked the back of his dick with her left hand as she ate his dick up as if she was hungry craving for it. She was sucking it vigoursly as if she was trying to suck the skin off of it, and shove it down her throat, and stroking it with her hand, all at the same damn time.

I love Ruby, I hope she never stop sucking my dick, Will thought to himself. At that instant moment she stopped took her mouth off his dick, and spit on his dick five times. Will couldn't believe she had just spit on him. She immediately started back sucking his dick. Will immediately felt how better it was after the moisture of the spit. Within seconds she paused and spit on his dick three more times back to back. Once she started back sucking on it the spit ran down her face which made her look like a sick dog foaming at the mouth.....

In no time flat Will was unleashing nut in her mouth as she drunk, and swallowed all of it like a champ.....

Afterwars Ruby laid on the couch on her back with her eyes shut thinking to herself like this guy getting ready to kill this pussy with that big ass dick, and he did just that.....

Will had her hollering, and screaming half the night. Before the night was done he even bust her the ass.....

After that night they promise not to let their sex interfere with their personal lives.....

CHAPTER 2

B lack entered Will's home.....
"Guess what happened," Black said. "What happened," Will asked? "I've been drafted to go fight in nam," Black said. Will paused, he couldn't believe what his ears were hearing.....

"That's sad," Will said in low tone of voice.

"Everything we've been through, all the efforts we put forth to be black powerful superior to the devils, and they pulled this stunt. They don't want to treat us as equals but now they want you to fight their war," Will said. "I aint going Imma skip town," Black said. "You can't skip town, that's a case, you gone to have to do a prison term when they catch up with you, that's a federal case I think they call it draft dodging or something like that," Will said. "So what would you do if they drafted you for war," Black asked? "I don't know, that's a good question. I might just go and kill up some of them Orientals. I think I'd rather try my luck on the battle field, than spend a long term in prison," Will said.....

Will, and Black paused for a moment in time as their minds was flooded with alot of unanswered questions, as they visualized the battle fields in Vietnam, death and destruction, and the past history of the white men hate, instead of loving.....

Within the upcoming days Black decided to go to fight the war in Vietnam.....

"Good evening my black, and beautiful people," Will said to the Black National Organization. "Good evening," the Black National Organization said back to Will simultaneously.....

"We were all design, and taught to be warriors to live, eat, and breed, on a militant mind settings, we have military minds.

That comes from ancient African tribes that's the way we survived and ruled our lands as soilders of war. Right now the white man has his own personal war going on, and forces us to fight it, due to their laws we have no other choice if called upon. No matter what happens don't let the white people tear you down mentally nor physically. Stick your chest out, and hold your head up, and concur all obstacles.....To the devils we are ugly to me we're all black, and beautiful," Will said full-heartedly.....After that meeting the Black Nationals begin to think more about the art of war.....

A couple weeks later Black was shipped of to Vietnam nervous, and worried about if he'll make it through alive. At this time Black was only twenty one years old, Will was only twenty years old, Ruby was twenty three. Majority of the Black Nationals were young, but they had the brains of people twice their age.....

Will decided to quit his job working for the white man. He felt as if he should practice what he preach. Will knew how to cut hair so he started cutting hair, as a hustle, and it paid of instantly.....

Once Black first made it to the U.S. soilders overseas he noticed that the soilders had to do extreme workouts. And he knew that his turn on the battle field was soon to come.....

After a period of training Black was sent to the battle field for war. He was nervous like never before in life, but he didn't let it show.

During his first few times on the battle fields he was lucky they didn't come across any enemy troops.....

His first time coming across enemy troops was one late night as the mosquitos constantly ate away at the soilders flesh as the hot dreary night seemed endlessly they walked across dry land as Black, as well as the other soilders hoped that they didn't step on a land mind which would be a painful death they made it to a small body of water which was only approximately two feet high.

They crossed the water, and made it to these short bushes. As they stood still in the water in which seperated them from dry land they looked in them, and seen a small camp of enemy troops.

The general gave signal with his hand for everyone to remain silent. Then the general used his fingers as a sign language giving orders in the way to attack.....

Black became even more nervous each second. He knew it was time for war, time to seperate the boys from the men.....

In no time the soilders were attacking enemy troops the sounds of on going rapid gun fire that flooded the sound waves of ears as grenades sounded off like rocket launchers. You could hear crying, screaming, yelling in different languages as death, and destructions became one.....

Once that battle was over the U.S stood triumphant, their was casulties of war on both sides. Majority of the casulties was that of the enemy troops. Those that the U.S. didn't put to death fled the camp.....

That night Black seen how prosperous the art of surprise could be......

Overtime Black experienced more episodes of being front line on the battle field, as soilders were constantly getting killed, Black started to like war fair.....

Overtime the other soilders begin to call Black, God. They nicknamed him God because everytime they'd go onto the battle field it seemed as if he had God on his side.....

Will, and Black stayed in constant contact mainly through letters, occasionally over the phone they'd talk.....

Black would tell Will how intense the war in nam was, and that it made their war games seem like a joke. Will told Black that the Black National were starting to rotate with the ViceLords. Black didn't like it, Black knew the ViceLords was a street gang.....

Will had met some of the outstanding members of ViceLords by cutting hair. Will had came to find out that they had some of the same exact concepts that Black Nationals had. They were even getting funded from the goverment to help uplift the black community, as a sign of thanks and reparation for blacks helping building this country which was long overdue.....

Will had been introduced to the minister of ViceLords. The minister instantly took a liking for Will because he was smart, and he showed the qualities of a leader.....

Overtime Will had did alotta dirt for the minister, Will would bring nightmares of death, and blood shed to reality for the minister.....

Within time Will, and majority of the Black Nationals became ViceLords, the minister made Will a five star universal elite.....

The king of ViceLord kept hearing good things about Will, and decided to start rotating with him a little. The king didn't rotate with to many people heavy; He loved people, but didn't trust no one.....

The king of ViceLord rotated with Will a little turned into alot. The king had never met someone so young, so thorough, and so dedicated to the upliftment of ViceLord, and the upliftment of the black community.....

At this point in time the ViceLords wasn't very deep but they we're on fast uprise. They mainly resided on the west side of Chicago. Their were a few in the surrounding suburbs, but they wasn't that deep.....

Will would go out, and do recruiting, and go out and provide knowledge, and finance, and whatever assistance he could to the black community.....

In no time flat Will was a supreme elite, and had jurisdiction to create gang literature that the ViceLords had to abide by. He also had the kings blessings to start his own branch of ViceLord if he decided he wanted to do that.....

Will worked on the literarure of ViceLord with the king, and the minister, and now had expectations in becomming the king of his own branch of Vicelord.....

Within the matter of months Will finally decided to start his own branch of ViceLord, his branch would be the Traveler ViceLords, T.V.L.....

Mainly but not all branches of ViceLord name derived from ancient African tribes.

The Traveler tribe was an ancient tribe from Africa that traveled to conquer other tribes but not in war, but using their brains to manipulate them to became as one. The traveler tribe would find out were slave ship were and go to kill white slave traders, sometimes they'd became successful, other times they'd come up unsuccessful slaughtered like animals, but those that would survive would continue on, on their missions.....

Their were many other ancient African tribes; the Mandego's, the Zulu's, the Shabazz, the Ghosts, but Will decided to use the Travelers name because they were more in the likeness of himself, and his beliefs.....

Will became the youngest king of any branch of ViceLord that ever existed.....

CHAPTER 3

A fter a year, and a half fighting in Vietnam Black's tour of duty was over, he was sent back home. He couldn't wait to touch the city streets again.....

Will went to pick up Black from the airport in one of his new cars. As they drove, and reminisced Will took Black through the areas were ViceLords dwelled Black was impressed.

Will took Black through the areas were they Travelers was, and Black couldn't believe how Will had blossomed in the streets while he was gone.

Black was impressed by Will's street growth, but still had the Black National concept embedded in his mind frame in which he didn't believe in Will's committing crimes.....

As the day turned to night Will took Black through one of his spots were they sold his dope at.

The spot was inside a small building, the dope fiends would go into the front door, and walk shortly to a door with a slot in it where the mail man would stick their mail in. The dope fiends would slide their money through that slot, and tell the people on the other side of the door exactly how many bags of dope they were interested in purchasing.

Will had someone in the front of the building on security so when the police come they could get rid of all the drugs, the money, and the gun. They'd get rid of it by quickly taking the front part of their vent off, and giving it to the neighbors, or they would just give it to one of the neighbors up stairs; the upstairs neighbors would drop a long cord down for them to load up their merchandise in when, and if the police ever came.....

Will, and Black sat across the street on top of the hood of Will's car checking out the business. Black couldn't believe how many customers were constantly coming, and how much money Will had to be making off all them customers.....

Many of the Black Nationals became Travelers. Those they didn't become Travelers still did things to uplift the black people in their on way, and time.

The Black Nationals never told anyone, about their involvement with Black National, or the war games they played. They all kept it secret, they didn't even tell the Travelers that wasn't initially Black Nationals, about Black Nationals.

From time to time the ex-Black Nationals continued to play war games.....

After they left Will dope spot they went to see all of the ex-Black Nationals. All of them was more than happy to see Black home from the war.....

The last ex-Black National member they went to see was Ruby. Tears of joy ran down Ruby's face; she was so happy that he made it home safe, because so many people was getting killed in that war.....

Will ended up dropping Black off at his moms house, and went to meet Ruby at his own house.....

Will went, and jumped in the shower, as Ruby sat on the couch with the tip of her finger in her mouth, sucking on it as if she was a shy teenage girl.

Will came out of the bathroom wearing a robe.

As Will robe dropped to the ground Ruby took off her dress in which she had no panties, no bra. She dropped to her knees, with purple lipstick on she gently placed Will's dick in her mouth begin humming and bobbing back, and forth doing her best to make him fill pleasure, and love through the art of dick sucking.....

Ruby, and Will had got real close, but they kept their loving a secret. Ruby loved Will as if was he an angel on earth. Will loved Ruby, adored her sex, but loved his real girlfriend even more.....

The next morning Will went to go pick up Black. Will took Black shopping for clothes, and took him to the car lot, and brought him a brand new Cadillac.....

As Black started driving the area in his new lac with Will in the passenger seat a dude named Smurf spotted them, and flagged them down. As they parked Smurf ran to the passenger seat, and Black easily raised down the window.....

"William, Dirt robbed me," Smurf said. "Don't never call me William, call me Will. My Dirt, Traveler Dirt robbed you," Will said. "Yep, he robbed me last night, I was looking for you all night, you was no where to be found. I was gone took care of my business, but I can't bring no hurt, harm, or danger to one of the ViceLord brothers, that's just like doing something to one of my family members," Smurf said. "How much he rob you for," Will asked? "A bill, and a quarter," Smurf said. "One, twenty-five," Will said, and then reached in his pocket pulled out a roll of money, counted out a hundred, and twenty five dollars, and gave it to Smurf.

"That's good the way you went about the situation. By us being black men, and ViceLords all of us are like family, well atleast we suppose to be like family. But T.V.L. is like my immediate family. Like I just said it's good that you went about it the way you did, 'cause if you ever cross me, and do something to anybody claiming T.V.L. it's gonna be killer clowns, guns that explode, and burning of eternal fire all at once as a rapture you must feel," Will said. "Come on William, I meant to say Will you know I wouldn't never do nothing to none of the Travelers," Smurf said. "I heard that slick shit you said out your mouth, talking about you was gonna handle your business. As long as I'm living, and breathing you or nobody else aint gone do shit to no Traveler, and if you do you aint gone get away with, so don't let me hear nothing like that come out your mouth again. Just meet me in the pool hall tomorrow around twelve thirty, or one, we gone enforce law on dirt," Will said. "Alright, I'll be there," Smurf said as he stepped away from the car, as Black pulled off.....

"I been knowing you for umteen years, and you make everybody call you Will. Whats wrong with calling you William, thats your full name," Black said. "Yes, you have known me for umteen years, and you been calling me Will for umteen years so just stick with it," Will said. "Well from now on call me God," Black said. "I'm not calling no other man God," Will said. "That's my name, they gave me that name while I was at war. They gave me that name because each time I'd go to battle I'd always stand triumphant, and I'd always make it back safe," Black said. "Okay then God," Will said possessing a big smile on his face.....

The next morning Will, God, and some of the ViceLords were in the pool hall shooting pool. Some where smoking cigars, while others were sipping cheap wine, while others were doing both. Will, didn't smoke or drink.....

While shooting pool Will kept looking out of the window to across the street. Will had a dime bag powder spot across the street. He kept looking over there observing the customers in, and out the indoor spot.....

Will winding up sending someone to get Dirt.....

About an hour later in comes Dirt through the pool hall door with one of the other Lords by his left side.....

"Will you was looking for me," Dirt said, as everyone in the pool hall stopped what they was doing, and got quiet.

Before Will answered Dirt, Dirt noticed Smurf standing over in the cut. Dirt immediately put his hand on his gun which was tucked in the waist of his pants. Then he gave Smurf a mean mugg, a cold stare, that of a villing from a nightmare.

Reality immediately came forth Dirt now knew what Will had wanted him for.

Although Dirt wasn't at all worried about Smurf pulling a stunt in the presence of Will he still clutched his gun just to let Smurf know if he got out of his body he'd be feeling the pain of bullets.....

Dirt step closer to Will as everyone including Smurf surrounded him.....

"This brother said you robbed him," Will said to Dirt. "Yeah I robbed him so what he aint no Traveler, he a Renegade, fuck 'em," Dirt said.....

All the other ViceLords that wasn't Travelers, and those that was frowned up in disgust.

"So what he aint no Traveler, he still a ViceLord. That's why I be telling ya'll to learn ya'll lit, then ya'll will know how to conduct ya'll self as ViceLords. Now if this brother would've came back and did something to you the Travelers would've had to murder the Renegades making them extinct going against the laws, and policies of ViceLords, and killing of our own black brothers," Will said as everyone remained speechless.....

139

"You gotta learn your lit, you in violation for baring arms against a member of ViceLord, disobeying the laws of ViceLord unity, and jeopardizing the body of ViceLord. Normally you suppose to get a minute for each charge, but by this being you first time in violation you gone get one minute from head to toe. Big C collect all the weapons from all the brothers in this room," Will said.

Big C was a Conservative ViceLord..... Always at meetings, or when a brother was in violation there was to be no weapons, because meetings, and violations were considered to be somewhat spiritual, sacret, and uplifting.....

Once Big C collected all the weapons from the brothers they all tucked in their shirts faced the east, bowed their heads closing their eyes, lifting their palms up.....

God stood in the cut watching everything amazed about how the ViceLords orchestrated things.....

Big C started to read the Statement of Love, "For you my brother my love begins at birth that has manifested itself throughout our heritage for the color of our skin which is black. For I am you, you are me. Our minds are for the same cause. Our efforts are for the same goals. Our souls bound for the same destination. Our lives are for the same new nation. For you my black brother I give my unity, my vitality, my undying love, almighty."

Once Big C was done reading the statement they all opened their eyes, and lifted their heads up.

Dirt stood against the wall.

Will looked at his watch then in a matter of seconds he gave Big C the go ahead, to violate Dirt.

Big C hit dirt in the face once, Dirt fell to the floor as Big C continued violating him for a minute.

After the violation Dirt stood to his feet body aching in slight pain, he shook each ViceLord hand, and then hugged them.

He shook hands, and hugged Will last. As he hugged Will, Will whispered in his ear, "learn your lit."

Afterwards Dirt, and the guy he came in the pool hall with left, and everybody started back playing pool, smoking, drinking, and laughing as if nothing never happen.....

God started to fall in love with the way the ViceLords did things.....

Will and God left the pool hall.....

"That was raw the way you did things back there, what was that, that guy was reading," God asked? "That was the Statement of Love, that's a piece of ViceLord literature, I'm the one that wrote it. Alot of ViceLord literature I wrote. I took alot of Black Nationals concept, and turned them into ViceLord concepts, and wrote it up in literature. Me or none of the others that was once Black National told the ViceLords about the Black National, I'll take that secret to the grave with me," Will said. "Literature I didn't even know gangs had literature," God said. "We not actually a gang we're a nation of people that's about the upliftment of black people. ViceLord is design to uplift the black people," Will said.....

God stopped at a stop sign and pulled out a cigarette, and set fire to it, and begin puffing.....

"You smoke cigarettes, you digging yourself an early grave. Black Nationals, are not to use drugs, alcohol, or smoke tobacco," Will said. "Black Nationals, don't suppose to commit crimes, unless they were hate crimes," God said, and then inhaled, and exhaled cigarette smoke. "But I commit crimes, for the uplifting of the community. I sell alotta drugs, but I take the money, and invest it into good things within the black community," Will said. "You tearing down the black community, selling them drugs," God said. "But if I don't sell it to them it's many others that will. But I promise you majority of my money is being invested into positive things that will make blacks prosperous in the future," Will said.....

Within the upcoming weeks God noticed that Will was serious, because he seen with his own eyes how Will helped blacks with the money he made off drugs. Will would give black churches large sums of money, provided blacks with places to live outside of the ghetto, help people with their bills, and donate money to schools for better, advanced books, so blacks could get a higher learning.....

God start to see with his own eyes how the goverment would help fund ViceLord; and that the ViceLord would do many things for the black community, such as help blacks find jobs, provide after school programs so that the kids could come there to study, and have fun, amongst other things.....

God started to spend time with ex-Black Nationals that had become Travelers he noticed that none of them were in the streets selling drugs, or committing crimes they were working in places of after school programs, drug treatment centers in the black community or in college working on degrees.....

In no time God became a Traveler. He went from having no status to a branch elite, that dictated only to Traveler ViceLords, to a universal elite that dictated to all Vicelords, then to the prince of T.V.L. And he earned his way up to that title......

The Traveler ViceLords, amongst other branches of ViceLords rapidly grew, and spreaded throughout the city, and to the surrounding suburbs.....

Will, and God both became amazed with numbers of membership growth. Many all through the westside of Chicago wherever you went you seen guys with their hats broke to the left flagging ViceLord.

God started to apply his military experience in Vietnam to the ViceLord structure. In the military when soilders were punished for minor things they'd only have to do a harsh workout. God put within ViceLord law that if a representitive of ViceLord did something minor to break law they wouldn't have to get violated physically, but they would only have to do a harsh work out. The king of all ViceLords, and the minister liked that concept.

The minister of ViceLord put Will and God in play to be his personal assistances with creating more diplomatic ViceLord literature.....

God wrote his first piece of Vicelord lterature called ViceLord Life:

ViceLord Life

In the scriptures of life let it be of the creators will and might to project and show liberty and disadvantages of life.
But let life be a test and delight.
Always honor, guard, and protect brothers and sisters of ViceLord life.
Let it be done here and on a positive note uplifting to show growth to others in life.
Be forever real, be forever ViceLord with-through, upon a ViceLords life.

God's second piece of literature he wrote was called Concepts of Men:

Concepts of Men

Policies, concepts, and the conduct of men.
Honoring the five points of the golden star to withstand.
Love, truth, peace, freedom, and justice to the blackmen.
Utilizing knowledge and intellect to advance.
Remain sane dealing with circumstances.
Uplifting the brothers as much as you can.
Obey the unity, policies, concepts, codes, and
conduct of being a black man.

After God wrote those first two pieces of lit, and put them in ViceLord literature the king of ViceLord, and the minister depending on God for more knowledgeable lit to add within ViceLord literature.....

The king of ViceLords, and the minister was honored to have Will, and God as outstanding members Of ViceLord; the king, and minister was amazed on how young, intelligent, and dedicated to uplifting the black community Will, and God was. What the king, and minister didn't know that Will, and God thrived off Black Nationalism long before they became Vicelords. What Will, and God didn't know was that the king, and minister was grooming them to be the king, and prince of not only the Travelers, but of all ViceLords.....

PREVIOUSLY PUBLISHED
URBAN NOVEL

QUEEN OF QUEENS

CHAPTER 1

"You sure this the right spot, man?" Slim asked.

"I'm positive this is the right spot. I wouldn't never bring you on no blank mission," Double J said.

With no hesitation, Double J kicked in the door and yelled, "Police! Lay the fuck down!"

Double J and Slim stormed into the crib with guns in hand, ready to fuck a nigga up if anybody made any false moves.

As they entered the crib, they immediately noticed two women sitting at the table. The women were getting ready to shake up some dope.

One of the women laid on the floor facedown, crying out, "Please, please don't shoot me."

She had seen many TV shows and movies in which the police kicked in doors and wrongfully thought an individual was strapped or reaching for a gun when they weren't, and the police hideously shot them, taking their lives from 'em.

The other woman tried to run and jump outta the window. Before she could do so, Double J tackled her down and handcuffed her.

Double J threw Slim a pair of handcuffs. "Handcuff her," Double J said.

As Slim began to handcuff the other chick, he began thinking, Where the fuck this nigga get some motherfucking handcuffs from?

The woman who was on the floor, crying, looked up and noticed that Slim wasn't the police.

"You niggas ain't no motherfucking police," she said.

Double J ran over and kicked her in the face, and busted her nose. "Bitch, shut the fuck up," Double J said.

She shut up, laid her head on the floor. As her head was filled with pain while tears ran down her face, with blood running from her nose, she silently prayed that this real-life nightmare would come to an end!

Simultaneously, Slim and Double J looked at the table filled with dope. Both Slim and Double J's mouths dropped. They'd never seen so much dope in their lives. Right in front of their eyes were one hundred grams of pure, uncut heroin.

Both women laid on the floor, scared to death. They'd never been so scared in their natural lives.

Double J went into the kitchen found some ziplock bags, came back and put the dope in them, and then stuffed the dope in the sleeves of his jacket 'cause it was too much dope to fit in his pockets.

"Man, we gotta hurry up. You know the neighbors probably heard us kick the door in," Slim said.

"The neighbors ain't heard shit 'cuz of all the fireworks going off. That's why I picked this time to run off in here, while the fireworks going off, so nobody won't hear us," Double J said.

"Shiit, they could've still heard us. The fireworks ain't going off inside the building," Slim said.

"Don't worry about it," Double J said.

"Lord, let's search the rooms before we leave. You know, if all this dope is here, it gotta be some guns or money in here somewhere," Double J said.

"Yep, Jo, I bet you it is," Slim said.

Double J walked over to the woman whose nose he busted, knelt, put a .357 to her ear, and clicked the hammer back. The woman heard the hammer click in her ear. She became so scared that she literally shit on herself.

"Bitch, I'ma ask you one time, where the rest of that shit at?" Double J asked in a deep hideous voice.

She began crying out and yelling, "It's in the closet, in the bottom of the dirty clothes hamper."

Double J went into the closet snatched all the clothes outta the hamper and found ten big bundles of money. He saw a book bag hanging in the closet, grabbed it, and loaded the money in it. Double J went back into the front room. Without second-guessing it, he shot both women in the back of their heads two times a piece.

Double J and Slim fled from the apartment building, got into their steamer, and smashed off. As Double J drove a few blocks away, Slim sat in the passenger side of the car, looking over at Double J, pissed off.

"Lord, why the fuck you shoot them hos?" Slim asked with hostility.

"Look at all the money and dope we got," Double J said.

"What that gotta do with it?" Slim asked.

"You know that that wasn't them hos shit. They was working for some nigga, and if that nigga ever found out we stuck him up for all that shit, he'd have a price on our heads. Now that the only people who knew about us taking that shit is dead, we don't gotta worry about that shit," Double J said.

Yeah, you right about that, Slim thought as he remained silent for a few seconds. "You just said something about dope and money. What money?" Slim asked.

"Look in the book bag," Double J said.

Slim unzipped the book bag, and it was as if he saw a million dollars. His mouth dropped, amazed by all the money that was in the book bag.

They hit the e-way and set fire to a lace joint as they began to think of all the things they'd be able to do with the money and dope.

Double J and Slim were two petty hustlers looking for this one big lick, and they finally got it. They had various hustles that consisted of robbing, car thieving, and selling a little dope. All their hustles revolved around King Phill. King Phill was a king of a branch of ViceLords, the Insane ViceLords (IVL). They'd rob, steal cars, and sell dope through King Phill, one way or the other.

Double J and Slim were basically King Phill's yes men. Whatever Phill would say or wanted them to do, they'd say yes to.

After forty-five minutes of driving, they parked the steamer on a deserted block where there were no houses, only a big empty park.

Double J began wiping off the inside of the car. Slim began to do the same.

"Make sure you wipe off everything real good. We don't wanna leave no fingerprints," Double J said.

"You ain't gotta tell me. The last thing I wanna do is get pinched for a pussy-ass stickup murder," Slim said.

Double J put the book bag on his back. They left the car, wiping off the inside and outside door handles, and they began walking to Double J's crib, which was about thirty minutes away.

"Lord, fire up one of them lace joints," Slim said.

"Here, you fire it up," Double J said as he passed the joint to Slim.

Slim instantly set fire to it. They walked swiftly to Double J's crib, continuously puffing on the lace joints. Once they made it halfway there, out of nowhere, Double J stopped in his tracks.

"What the fuck you stop for?" Slim asked.

"Lord, we gotta get rid of that car," Double J said.

"Why?" Slim asked.

"'Cuz like you said, we don't wanna get pinched for no stickup murder. If somebody seen that car leave the scene of the crime and they tell the police and the police find the car and dust it for fingerprints and find one fingerprint that matches one of ours, we booked. We'll be sitting on death row saying what we should've, would've, and could've done," Double J said.

"How we gone get rid of it?" Slim asked.

"Here, take my gun and bookbag and meet me at my crib. My girl there, she'll let you in," Double J said.

"You still didn't answer my question," Slim said.

"What's that?" Double J asked.

"How we gone get rid of the car?" Slim asked.

"Don't worry about it. I got it," Double J said.

"Let's get rid of it together," Slim said.

"Naw, man, we need to make sure the money and dope is safe, and we need to get these hot-ass guns off the streets," Double J said.

"Where is the dope?" Slim asked.

Double J reached into his sleeves, pulled out the dope, and handed it all to Slim as they departed and went their separate ways.

I hope this nigga don't get caught fucking around with that car, Slim thought.

Double J went back to the car, looking for something to use to set it on fire. He ended up finding some charcoal fluid in the trunk of the car, squeezed all the fluid out of the bottle all over the car, struck a match, and threw it on the car as it instantly began burning. Double J took off running. He ran halfway home and walked the other half.

Once Double J made it home, before he could even knock on the door or ring the doorbell, Slim opened the door. Double J rushed in nervously and slammed the door behind himself and frantically locked it.

"Nigga, what the fuck took you so long?" Slim asked.

"What took me so long? Shiiit, I ran halfway back, but anyway, I took care of the business. I burned the car up," Double J said.

"How much dough we got?" Double J asked.

"I don't know. I ain't even open the book bag up, I was waiting to you get here," Slim said.

"See that's why I fuck with you. Anybody else would've played me for some of the money and dope," Double J said.

"You my nigga. I wouldn't never try to get over on you. To keep it real, you didn't even have to take me on the lick with you," Slim said.

They went into the bathroom, locked the door, and began counting the money. Each bundle of money was a G.

"Damn, Lord, we got ten stacks and all this dope," Slim said.

"How we gone get rid of all this dope?" Double J asked.

"We gone sell it in grams," Slim said.

"Naw, man, we need to sell it in bags. We'll make more money selling it in bags. The only problem is where we gone sell it at. You know anywhere we try to open up at, they gone close us down," Double J said.

"We gone sell it in the hood," Slim said.

"Stop playing! You know damn well we dead in the hood. You know if we open up in the hood, they gone close us straight down," Double J said.

"We gone have to go through Phill," Slim said.

"Yeah, we'll get up with Phill tomorrow," Double J said.

"Man, don't tell nobody where we got the dope from."

"Nigga, do I look like a lame to you? What the fuck I look like, telling somebody about what we did," Slim said.

"I'm finna go to sleep. You might as well spend a night," Double J said.

"Yeah, I might as well spend a night," Slim said.

"I'll holla at you in the morning. I'm sleepy as hell," Double J said as he started to yawn.

Slim went and lay on the couch in the living room. Double J went into his bedroom, undressed down to his boxers and T-shirt, and got into bed with his wife, who he assumed was asleep. As Double J pulled the covers back, he noticed that his wife was in bed asshole-naked. I'm glad I married her, Double J thought while enjoying the view.

Slim and Double J stayed awake for a little while, thinking about the money they had and the profit they was going to make off the dope. As Double J closed his eyes to go to sleep, he felt his wife's hands gently slipping into his boxers, rubbing his dick.

"I thought you were asleep," Double J said.

"I ain't sleep. I was just lying here thinking about you," she said. She continued rubbing on his dick.

"Now you know you can't be rubbing on my dick without any lubrication. That shit don't feel good when you do it with dry hands," Double J said.

She got up and squeezed a little Jergens in the palm of her hand as he slipped his boxers off and lay back on the bed. She grabbed his dick firmly, began lathering it up with the lotion, and jagging him off at the same time.

As she thoroughly jagged him off, he pumped her hand until his nut unleashed on her titties, and she began rubbing the nut around on her titties as if it was baby oil or lotion. She then took his dick into her mouth, gobbling it and the lotion in all, swirling her tongue around it and sucking on it as if she was trying to suck some sweet nectar out of it.

Once it got rock hard, she began deep throating it, choking herself with his dick while rubbing on her own clitoris roughly while humming. In no time flat, he was releasing a load of nut down her throat. She stood, wiped her mouth, and slightly began growling. She then got on top of him and played with his dick for a few seconds until it got back hard.

She looked him in his eyes, as she grabbed his dick firmly and shoved it in her pussy, and began smiling. She began riding it slowly to get her pussy totally wet, while he grabbed her ass cheeks, guiding her movements.

Once her pussy got wet, he began slamming his dick in and out of her, enjoying the tightness of her moist pussy. She clawed his chest, moaning in the midst of pleasure and pain; she liked when it hurt.

It felt so good to him that every time he'd slam his dick up in her pussy, it felt like he was actually nutting.

As Double J began to nut, she was cumming simultaneously. As he began to slam his dick in and out her pussy rougher and harder, she began fucking him back. It was like a rodeo show as their orgasms exploded.

"Get up. Get on the bed so I can hit it from the back," Double J said.

She got on all fours on the bed. Double J got on his knees right behind her and began squeezing and rubbing her big brown pretty ass cheeks.

"Tell me you love me before you start fucking me," she said.

"I love your hot ass," he said. Double J then rammed his dick in her hot pussy, gripping her ass cheeks and slamming his dick in and out her pussy hard and fast while admiring the way her ass cheeks bounced. In no time, he was letting another nut explode in her pussy.

"Let me suck it," she said in a low seductive tone.

"Hold on, let me roll up a joint," Double J said.

"You know that I don't like the smell of lace joints. Why you got to lace your weed with cocaine? Why you can't smoke regular weed like everybody else?" she said.

Double J began smiling and looking her straight in the eyes. "Well, I'll smoke a regular joint just for you," Double J said. He rolled up a regular joint with only weed in it, set fire to it as she got on her knees with an aim to please.

As he inhaled and exhaled the potent weed smoke, she simultaneously sucked his dick, utilizing a suction method sucking mainly the tip thoroughly. The potent effect of the weed combined with her superb suction method and the moisture of her mouth felt so good that within seconds he released a glob of nut in her face.

He finished smoking his joint, and both of them lay on the bed. "You must really been wanting to fuck," Double J asked.

"I been thinking about you all day at work. I had to take off work because I creamed in my panties daydreaming about your dick going in and out my pussy and mouth. I been sitting in the house all day waiting on you," she said.

I done married a freak, Double J thought

They began to tell each other how much they loved each other and how their lives wouldn't be the same without each other, before both of them fell into a deep sleep.

The next morning, after Double J's wife had gone to work, Double J and Slim sat at the kitchen table eating breakfast, reminiscing about the stickup and the murders.

They glorified and celebrated the stickup and the murders as if they were professional athletes who just won a championship game or as if they had won the lottery.

It's sad how bloodshed make others glad. But this life some live in as thugs consist of no love. Other people were brought up to increase the peace and strive to earn college degrees, and live the American dream. But those who live the street life thrive on death and destruction. They rob, steal, and kill with no discretion, and glorify others' names who do the same.

"Hurry up and finish eating so we can go holla at Phill," Double J said.

"I'm already finished," Slim said.

"Well, empty the rest of that shit that's on the plate in the garbage and put that plate in the sink," Double J said.

Slim emptied the rest of the food in the garbage, put the plate in the sink, and went and grabbed the book bag.

"Naw, we gone leave the dope and shit here, unless you wanna take your half to your house," Double J said.

"It's cool, I'll leave it here," Slim said.

As they rode up the block in the hood where Phill was, they noticed many of the Insanes on Phill's security as usual.

Once they made it to where Phill was, Phill began smiling, 'cuz he was happy to see them. He needed them to take care of some business for him.

King Phill was a pretty boy. Stood about six feet five, half-Latino, half-black, with naturally curly black hair in his midtwenties. Those who didn't know Phill personally would've never believed that he was a king of a large street gang. King Phill looked like a pretty boy college student.

"Park the car. I need to holla at ya'll," Phill said.

They parked and got out to holla at him.

"I need ya'll to get some steamers for me," Phill said.

"We ain't on no car-thieving shit right now. We need your assistance on some other shit," Double J said.

"What ya'll need?" Phill asked.

"Let's step away from everybody. It's personal," Slim said.

As they stepped away from everybody else, Phill began trying to figure out what Double J and Slim wanted. Maybe they finna ask for some shit, Phill thought.

"Phill, we got some dope we need to get off," Double J said.

"What you talking about?" Phill asked.

"We need to pop it off in the hood," Slim said.

"What ya'll talking about, opening up a dope spot in the hood?" Phill asked.

"That's exactly what we're talking about," Slim said.

"You know ya'll can't work in the hood if ya'll ain't a five-star universal elite," Phill said.

"I told him," Double J said.

"Well, make us universal elites," Slim said.

Phill began laughing. "I don't just give out status like that. I ain't one of these phony-ass niggas that let people buy status. You gotta earn it fucking with me," Phill said.

Slim looked at Phill like he was crazy. "Earn it? All the shit we do for you and for the hood while them niggas you made universal elites be in the Bahamas some-motherfucking-where! We be doing all the shootings for the hood and all type of other shit for you and the hood," Slim said.

"Yeah, you do got a point, 'cuz ya'll do stand on nation business. This what I'm going to do for ya'll. I'ma let ya'll work in the hood under my name, but ya'll gotta pay," Phill said.

"How much we gotta pay?" Slim asked.

"That depends on how much dope ya'll got," Phill said.

"We got ten grams," Double J said. He was lying.

"Ten grams? That ain't shit. Ya'll work them ten grams for two or three weeks outta Argale park. In two or three weeks, ya'll should've at least doubled or tripled them ten grams. Once ya'll do, ya'll gotta give me a stack every week," Phill said.

Double J and Slim looked at each other smiling, knowing it was finna be on.

"A stack a week. We got you. We'll holla at you. I gotta go pick my girl up from work." Double J said. He was lying.

As Double J and Slim got into the car and rode off, listening to Al Green's "Love and Happiness." They were happier than a kid on Christmas Day.

CHAPTER 2

Three Days Later

"How much is that small black digital scale?" Double J asked the cashier.

"That one right there is a hundred dollars. But I'd recommend this white one right here if you're going to be weighing things over twenty-eight grams. A lot of customers usually buy that small black one, then later on down the line, the same customers come back and buy a bigger one, which is a waste of money to me," the woman cashier said.

"How much do the white one cost?" Slim asked.

"Two hundred," the cashier said.

"We'll take it," Slim said.

"Will that be it?" the cashier asked.

"Naw, we need five bottles of Dormin and a bundle of them little black baggies right there and two of them mac spoons," Slim said.

As other customers walked into the small record store, the cashier paused and began covering up the small area where contraband was being sold.

"Thomas, can you service the new customers?" the female cashier said to her coworker.

"Wait 'til these customers leave, then I'll give ya'll, ya'll items," the female cashier said to Double J and Slim.

"Ya'll sell scales, baggies, and all type of shit to everybody in the city, and now you wanna act like it's top secret," Slim said.

"Yeah, we do supply a lot of people with contraband, but those are only the people that come in here asking for it. We can't have contraband on display, because it's all types of people that come in here. A person might come in here with their kids. Or an off-duty police officer might come in here to buy some records. And if they see all this contraband on display, they'll report our ass to the city. We won't lose our store or anything like that, but we'll have to pay a healthy fine," the cashier said.

Within minutes, the other customers purchased their records and left the store.

"Your total will come out to three hundred seventy-five dollars," she said.

Slim paid her, and they left the store.

Once they made it to Double J's crib, they immediately weighed the dope for the first time.

"Damn, Lord, we got a hundred grams! I thought it'll be about fifty grams," Slim said.

"Yeah, me too," Double J said.

"Aw, we finna put up numbers if this shit is a bomb," Slim said.

"Showl is," Double J said.

"Why did you buy baggies instead of aluminum foil?" Double J asked.

"'Cuz we gone put the dope in the baggies. We don't need no aluminum foil," Slim said.

"But we need to put it in the aluminum foil so it can stay fresh," Double J said.

"Once we put it in the baggies then put some thick clear tape on the baggies, the dope will stay fresh," Slim said.

"We need to find us a connect on some quinine," Double J said.

"Naw, we ain't gone put no quinine or none of that other crazy shit on the dope. We either gone use dorms or sell it with no mix on it at all. We gone put three pills on each gram of dope," Slim said.

"How many grams we gone bag up the first time?" Double J asked.

"We gone bag up ten grams first and put it out there and see what it do. You know we can't bag up to much, 'cuz if it don't sell quick enough, it'll fall off," Slim said.

"That's my point exactly. That's why I ask," Double J said.

Double J weighed out ten grams on the scale. Then Double J and Slim opened up thirty dorms, which were actually capsules. Double J and Slim then grabbed two playing cards apiece and began mixing the dope with the dorms.

"How many mac spoons we gone use?" Double J asked.

"We gone give up two macs for a sawbuck and see how that go first. If the dope is a bomb, we gone drop down to one mac spoon or a mac and a half. That all depends on how good the dope is. And if it's real good, we gone put more dorms in it," Slim said.

Double J and Slim grabbed a mac spoon apiece and began measuring the dope and putting it in the bags.

"I got some thick clear tape in my room, in the closet," Double J said.

"Wait 'til we get finished before you go get it," Slim said.

After about an hour and a half, they'd finally finished bagging up the dope.

"Let's count it up to see how much we bagged up," Double J said.

"We gone put twelve blows in a pack. Whoever sells the pack gets twenty dollars and turns us in a hundred," Slim said.

"How much we gone pay people to run the joint?" Double J asked.

"We ain't worried about that right now. We gone run the joint ourselves. Once it picks up, then we'll put people in play to run the joint. We'll worry about what we gone pay them when that time comes," Slim said.

As they sat at the table counting up the dope, Slim began to wonder who they were going get to work the packs.

"Shiiit, who we gone get to work the joint?" Slim asked.

"My lil cousins gone work the joint. They been sweating me for the last couple days about when we gone open up the joint so they can work. They juveniles, so if they catch a case, they mommas can just sign them out from the police station," Double J said.

Once they finished counting the dope up, it came out to twenty packs and seven odds. They bagged up $2,070, not including the two blows in each pack for the pack workers to get paid.

Slim began doing the mathematics in his head. "So if we got two stacks off ten grams, then we gone get at least twenty stacks off of the whole hundred grams," Slim said.

"Shiit, we gone get more than that if the dope is a bomb and if it can take more than three pills a gram," Double J said.

"Yep, showl is. Go grab the tape outta the closet," Slim said. When he came back with the tape, Slim examined it. "Yeah, Joe, this tape perfect," Slim said.

They put twelve bags on a strip of tape then put another strip of tape over the bags. They put the tape over the bags in order for the dope to stay fresh, and so none of the workers wouldn't dip into the bags.

Double J and Slim grabbed the dope and a .45 automatic and went to pick up Double J's cousins and set up shop in Argale Park. They posted up at the corners and in the park. One of Double J's cousins walked through the hood, telling all the dope fiends that they were passing out free dope in Argale Park. They dope fiends rushed to the park and spread the word. Two niggas who stood in the park, Double J's cousins, were passing out the samples to the dope fiends. A couple of hours later, the park was filled with dope fiends shopping for dope.

Double J and Slim couldn't believe how fast and how many dope fiends were coming to buy dope. Judging by the large amount of dope fiends who were coming to buy dope so soon, Double J and Slim knew they had some good dope.

"Damn, Lord, look how many dope fiends waiting in line to shop," Slim said.

"That's 'cuz the dope fiends that we gave samples to went and told everybody that we got good dope. Word of mouth travels," Double J said.

Within two days and one night, Double J and Slim sold the whole hundred grams.

"Lord, who we gone buy some more dope from?" Slim asked.

"That's a good question," Double J said.

As they continued to smoke and ride through the hood, they remained silent, trying to figure out who they'd start buying weight on the dope from.

"We gone have to start buying from Phill," Double J said.

"Phill got good dope, but it ain't a bomb," Slim said.

"How you know? You don't even use dope," Double J said.

"I can tell from the numbers his dope spots put up. His spots put up little numbers, but they ain't all that," Slim said.

"Who else we gone buy dope from? We gone have to get it from Phill," Double J said.

"Ride through Lexington and see if he out there," Slim said.

As they made it to Lexington, they saw Phill standing on the corner with a gang of niggas standing around him for his security.

"A Phill, check it out, Lord," Slim said.

Phill walked toward them smiling.

"Where's my money at?" Phill said.

"What money?" Slim asked.

"My g, what else? Money. I heard ya'll been tipping outta the park," Phill said.

"We'll get the money we owe you a little later on," Slim said.

"It ain't even been a whole week," Double J said.

"So what? I want my money ya'll been tipping," Phill said.

"A'ight we got you," Double J said.

"How much you'll sell us twenty-five grams of dope for?" Slim asked.

"Three thousand," Phill said.

"That's kinda high, ain't it?" Double J said.

"Naw, that's low. Anybody else I charge one fifty a gram. I'm only charging ya'll like one twenty-five a gram. At one twenty-five a gram, twenty-five grams suppose to come out to thirty-one twenty-five, but I just said an even three stacks. I ain't tripping over a hundred and twenty-five dollars. Look, right, I got shit I gotta do. Is ya'll gone need that twenty-five grams or not?" Phill asked.

"Yeah, we need it now," Double J said.

"I can't get it for ya'll right now, but I'll have somebody get it for ya'll later," Phill said.

"We gone have the g we owe you when you sell us the twenty-five grams, so we'll bring the whole four thousand with us," Slim said.

"I gotta go. I'll holla at ya'll later on," Phill said.

"Make sure we get them twenty-five grams today. Our joint is outta work," Slim said.

"I got ya'll. Don't worry about it," Phill said.

"A'ight, we'll holla at you," Slim said.

Later on that day, they were sitting in Double J's crib, chilling, when they got a call from Phill telling them that he was going to send his guy John over with the twenty-five grams, and that they needed to make sure the four stacks was counted up right before they gave it to John.

Once John delivered the twenty-five grams, they went straight to Double J's kitchen table and started bagging up.

"How many pills we gone use?" Double J asked.

"We gone use three first, to see how the dope fiends like it with three in it," Slim said.

Both of them began opening up the seventy-five capsules and dumping the inside of the dorms on the table, on top of the twenty-five grams.

"Lord, if this dope is any good, we finna be getting money like never before. Fuck spending our money. We need to stack our shit and get into some real estate, then we can leave the dope game alone," Slim said.

"Yeah, I agree with you on that. You know all these other niggas be spending their shit, then when it comes time for bound money, they can't even bound out for ten or fifteen stacks," Double J said.

As they continued mixing up the dope, they both imagined of riches.

They next day, they put the dope on their joint, and to their surprise, the dope fiends loved it.

They finished that twenty-five grams in one day, and was right back at Phill's buying fifty grams this time. Phill was a player who liked to see niggas doing good getting money, so he sold them fifty grams for fifty-five hundred.

Once they put that fifty grams out, their they thought it would slow down some because the dope fiends would know from the last twenty-five grams that they ain't selling the same dope they had originally when they first opened up.

Double J and Slim sat back at the end of the park, admiring the view of the customers swarming to buy dope. It was as if every time the pack worker would bring out a new pack, the dope fiends would swarm on him like flies to shit.

"How the hell is our joint tipping like this with Phill's dope, and his joint ain't putting up numbers like ours?" Double J asked.

"That 'cuz Phill and a lot of these other niggas be putting that crazy shit on they dope. That's why I told you we ain't gone use nothing but dorms. Phill nam still checking a bag, but their turnover rate is slower," Slim said.

Within a month, Double J and Slim were the men. Their joint was putting up numbers. They bought new Cadillacs, new sports cars, and all. Their team of workers constantly grew. Hos coming from everywhere were trying to get with them. Throughout it all, they continued to buy dope from Phill.

CHAPTER 3

O ne hot sunny day, Double J was simply bending blocks in the hood, listening to Al Green, puffing on joints that weren't laced with cocaine when he saw her from the back in those jeans.

Damn, this ho thick as hell, Double J thought.

He pulled up to her. Once he saw her face, he became disappointed. Aw, this Cynthia dope fiend ass, he thought.

Cynthia immediately opened the passenger-side door and just jumped in his car.

"Take me to your spot to get some dope," she said.

"I got a few bags in my pocket," Double J said.

"What are you doing, riding around with dope in your pocket?" Cynthia asked.

"What else am I doing with dope in my pocket?" Double J said sarcastically.

"I didn't know you shoot dope," Cynthia said.

"Tell somebody, and I'll kill you," Double J said.

They drove to a quiet block on the outskirts of the hood, pulled over, and parked.

Double J gave Cynthia the dope to hook it up and put in the needle.

Once she hooked the dope up and put it in the needle, she tried handing the needle to Double J.

"Naw, you go ahead. Ladies first," Double J said.

With her right hand, she shot dope into the veins of her left arm. As her eyes rolled in the back of her head, her entire body felt as if it were taken to a whole other planet. Afterward, she passed the needle to Double J.

With his right hand, he shot dope into the veins of his left arm. As Barry White's song "I'm Never Gone Leave Your Love" played on the radio, Double J felt as if he was soaring above the clouds.

Afterward, Double J dropped Cynthia off at home and went and met Slim at his crib to shake up some dope.

"I bought a hundred grams instead of fifty," Slim said.

"That's cool," Double J said.

"Start busting the dorms down. I gotta go use the bathroom. My stomach fucked up from smoking all them lace joints," Slim said.

Slim came out the bathroom and saw Double J sitting at the table, nodding and scratching.

"Damn, nigga, you look like you done had a dope," Slim said.

"Naw, man, I'm just sleepy," Double J said.

So they both began busting the dorms down.

Double J kept scratching and nodding at the table.

This nigga fucking around with dope, Slim thought.

"Lord, tell the truth. Ain't you getting high?" Slim asked.

"Nigga, you know damn well I been getting high ever since you've known me," Double J said.

"Nigga, you know what I'm talking about. Is you fucking with dope?" Slim said.

Double J paused for a little while. "Yeah, I fuck around with the dope a little," Double J said.

"What made you turn into a dope fiend?" Slim asked.

"I use to be seeing how dope fiends look after they get high. Some of them looked like it's the best feeling in the world. Some of them be looking like they're walking on the clouds or some shit. Then I start to see how the dope fiends do whatever it takes to get money for dope. That made me want to try some even more, 'cuz I knew it had to be some good shit. Once I tried it, it felt like heaven on Earth. No lie, I'ma be a dope fiend forever. I'ma get high 'til I die," Double J said.

Slim looked at Double J with a smirk on his face, thinking, This nigga done lost his mind.

"Niggas always trying to belittle dope fiends, when they get high they motherfucking self off all types of shit. A drug addict is a drug addict. It don't matter if you smoke weed, lace weed, toot cocaine, toot dope, or shoot dope—you still a drug addict," Double J said.

"I can agree with you on that 'cuz I smoke more lace joints than some people use dope," Slim said.

"We gone have to start paying somebody to bag up this dope. This shit a headache," Slim said.

"Straight up," Double J said.

In the days that followed, Slim began to admire how suave Double J was as he was high off dope. As he walked, talked, drove, ate, smoked cigarettes, every way he maneuvered was super cool when he was drunk off dope.

Before long, Slim began asking Double J a gang of questions on how it felt to be high off dope.

"You steady asking me about how it feels to be high off dope. My best answer is you won't know how it feels until you try it," Double J said.

"I'm scared of needles," Slim said.

"You ain't gotta shot it. You can toot it. But it ain't nothing look shooting it. As that dope run up your veins, it's the best high you'll ever experience," Double J said.

Slim was still hesitant to try dope. He let his pride get in the way. He knew certain people looked down on dope fiends.

A couple of days later at a club, with these two lesbian chicks he dated and paid for sex, he began wanting to try some dope again. The lesbian chicks Tricey and Reese did it all besides dope. They snorted lines of cocaine, smoked lace joints and regular weed, and smoked leaf.

After downing a few drinks at the club. The girls sat at the table, snorting line after line of cocaine secretly, not in the public's eye.

"Damn, ya'll gone fuck around and OD," Slim said.

"That's only if you use dope. You ain't gonna find to many people OD'ing off cocaine, although you can OD off cocaine," Reese said.

"Have ya'll ever fucked around with dope before?" Slim asked.

"Hell naw, we ain't no motherfucking dope fiends," Tricey said.

"Shiiit, ya'll get high off everything else," Slim said.

"Everything besides dope," Tricey said.

"I heard that dope is the best high known to mankind," Slim said.

"Yeah, me too. But it takes control over your body. You gotta have it or your body won't be able to function right. And I heard the sickness is a motherfucker," Tricey said.

"I wanna snort a line or two to see how it feels," Slim said.

"So you wanna be a dope fiend?" Reese said sarcastically.

"Naw, I just wanna snort just one bag of dope to see how it feels. I want ya'll to snort it with me," Slim said.

"Hell naw," Reese said.

"Let's all three of us try it together," Slim said.

For almost an hour at the club, Slim tried convincing the girls to snort a bag of dope with him, and it worked. Slim pulled up to his dope spot.

"Tyrone, who working, Lord?" Slim asked.

"Ush working," Tyrone said.

"Why don't I see nobody shopping?" Slim asked.

"It's kinda slow right now, but you can best believe it'll be a gang of customers in line in no time," Tyrone said.

"Go get me three bags of dope, and hurry up, Lord," Slim said.

Tyrone rushed to go get three bags from Ush and brought it right back to the car. Slim took the dope and smashed off.

Slim parked a few blocks over from his joint. He tore open a bag of dope with his teeth and laid it on one of the girls' cigarette box. He tore a piece of the paper off his matchbox. He scooped up half the dope and snorted it like a pro. He sat the Newport box on the dash and leaned back in his seat to feel the total effect of the dope.

Within seconds, Slim had his door opened as he bent over, throwing up his guts.

If that shit gone have me throwing up like that, I don't even want none, Tricey thought.

After Slim finished throwing up, he snorted the other half of the dope off of the Newport box. He lay back in his seat and relaxed for minutes and began to feel the effect of being drunk off dope. The girls then snorted their bags.

As they lay there, high, they all thought within their own silent minds that dope was the best drug known to man.

Slim and both women wound up in a motel room. Slim's dick stayed on hard all the while. Slim had heard of the dope dick but didn't know that it was this intense.

For the entire week that followed, Slim snorted dope and smoked laced joints each day.

One morning as Slim went home, he got into it with his main girlfriend. She was tired of him spending nights out and cheating on her. She threw some hot coffee on him and swung at him a few times, leaving him with a few minor scars on his face. Slim stormed out the house and went to his joint.

Slim pulled on the joint, got two bags of dope, and pulled around the corner to blow them. He pulled back around to his joint sat on the hood of his car smoking a lace joint, thinking of all the good times, and the bad times he had, had with his girlfriend. He was still a little pissed off 'cuz she put her hands on him.

Double J pulled off, laughing.

"So I see you having problems with your girl," Double J said.

"How you know?" Slim asked.

"'Cuz I see you sitting there, faced all scratched up, looking crazy. I know you ain't let no nigga do it to you, because we'll be in war right now," Double J said.

Slim tossed the duck of the joint on the ground, bailed in with Double J, and Double J pulled off.

"Man this ho crazy. As soon as I walked through the door, she got to throwing shit, hollering, screaming, and swinging," Slim said.

"We all go through problems with women. That's been going on since the beginning of time," Double J said.

"Pull over for a minute. I need to take care of some business," Slim said.

Double J pulled over and put the car in park.

"What, you gotta piss or something?" Double J asked.

"Naw, I need to take care of something else," Slim said.

Slim pulled out his pack of cigarettes, then pulled out a bag of dope, opened it with his teeth, and poured it on the cigarette box. Double J remained silent. He couldn't believe what he was seeing. Slim then pulled out a small piece of a straw and snorted the entire bag of dope. Double J just sat there, looking at him like he was crazy.

Slim fired up a cigarette, looked at Double J, and asked, "Is my nose clean?"

"Yes, it's clean," Double J said.

"I can't believe you sat there and snorted a bag of dope after you been getting down on me after you found out I was getting high," Double J said.

"I been seeing how good you been looking when you high off dope. It be like you be walking on clouds or some shit, and I wanted that feeling. So I tried it, and I love it," Slim said.

"I told you it was a bomb, especially if you shoot it," Double J said.

Double J began smiling and pulled off, listening to Barry White's song "Ecstasy" as they drove to the mall.

Once they made it inside the mall, Slim became so happy at seeing all the hos there that he forgot all about what he and his girl had gone through earlier.

Slim wound up getting a gang of numbers from ho's.

When they entered this one shoe store, Slim couldn't take his eyes off this white chick. She was raw as hell. She was about five feet six, 140 pounds, a redhead, with black eyeliner around her hazel blue eyes, and red lipstick. She looked like a model or some shit. Slim decided to walk over and strike up a conversation with her.

Slim came to find out that her name was Angie. She lived on the north side of town. Twenty years of age with no boyfriend, no kids, or none of that. They exchanged numbers and went their separate ways.

All the rest of the day, Slim couldn't stop thinking of Angie. She just looked so good to him.

Slim went home that night and made up with his girl, and they got down from break-up to make-up sex.

Slim had never been with a white woman before but always wanted one. The next day, Slim wound up giving Angie a call. He thought she was gonna be on some phony shit, but he was wrong. She was real cool.

Slim and Angie starting hanging out together damn near every day. One of the things Slim liked about Angie was that she genuinely liked him for him. She wasn't like the other women that he'd fucked around with. They were only interested in money one way or the other. Angie wasn't.

Within a couple months, Slim left his main girl for Angie and moved in with her.

Within several months, Double J and Slim found their dope habits increasing. Having to spend more money to support their habits, for guns, for money on bonding their guys outta jail, and for having to pay more bills. This fortune and fame wasn't all what it seemed.

UPCOMING POETRY BOOKS

LOVE VOLUME 1

1. ON TOP

On top loving non stop
around the clock.
A system of loving that rocked.

On top we'd watch the sunrise
making plans for the new days that shall flock.

On top they'll be love non stop.

2. IN CHRIST

In Christ things will become.
Became unified as one.
Divided eternal life and death
forgiving for sins God's son.
Love shall become the tree
of love to become.
All things in the dark shall shine
like the light of Christ,
believe in him and it shall become.

3. PART OF MY IDENTITY

Part of my identity.
Spiritually.
Religiously.
Liberty.
Always have a place in my
heart part of me, part of my identity.

4. THANKS FOR BLESSINGS

Thank God for his many blessings.
Love of life less stressing.
Thank God for living life still living
in each timely session.

5. REACHED

Reached sought and seeked.
Love that stood through the distance
reached.
From head to feet reached.
Sweet like the nectar from strawberry or peach.
Love was made famous would be wherever i was at reached.

6. BETTER IMAGES

Better images crossing lines
of schrimage pacing as a turtle
to the line of finish.
Love that had no ending.
Constant visions of her,
the best images.

7. SEVEN

Her parents named her seven,
because of one through seven she was a blessing.
Two because she was wonderful a guru.
Three because she gave them a sense of hope,
a way to let love,
and life be free.
Four because she'd bring forth life which was beautiful,
and they wanted to give birth to more.
Five is because she had vibrant vibe that
kept hope alive.
Six was because she kept them wanting
better lives in the mix.
They named her seven because she was
a blessing from Heaven.

8. AT LAST

At last love came to pass.
The unveiling of a veil, a mask.
Loves gonna last.
Came like a sudden shocking blast.
At last love came to pass.

9. SEEDS THAT GREW

Who'd ever knew from a simple planted
seed something beautiful and new grew.
Memorable melodies from a flute.
The intellect of study groups.
Love and respect that was always there and due,
and was true.
She was colorful, wonderful, beautiful, and all brand new.
A seed that grew.

10. I Wish I Had

I wish I had someone like me.
Someone that peacefully roam the streets.
A poet like me that write poetry.
Someone that cries out,
and pray for those locked
behind bars to be free.
Interesting in hunger to feed,
helping those in need.
Instead of poverty, thinking positively.
Giving visions, tools of life, keys.
Someone that's heart, and mind is free.
I wish I had that special lady to be;
someone who is just like me.

LOVE VOLUME 2

1. OTHER SIDE OF TOWN

She lived on the other side of town.
I'd travel the distance to see her,
I loved having her around.
She made my love 360 degrees as our
love goes round, and round.
Her ex lost, I'm glad I found.
Loving by the pounds.
She was thoroughbred,
never wore any make up, red noses,
and big Bozo shoes like the clowns.
She already knew that each time we meet it was going down.
Laughs with no frowns.
It was like a vacation outta town.
Her, I loved being around can't
wait to take the ride on the other
side of town.

2. NEVER LEAVE ALONE

A could never leave you alone.
While your at work or just away
from home I send you text messages
knowing that my love for you is long.
Wine, roses, and dinner is waiting
for you when you get home.
I stay showing love I could never leave
you alone.
To me we are in the same like a clone.
I can't see me without you on my own,
we gotta be together and I could never
leave you alone.

3. HER LOVE

Her kisses granted wishes.

Her smile lasted a long while.

Her love came from Heavens above.

4. HIGH PERFORMANCE

High hopes, high performance.
Loving was enormous.
Helping me get through the storming.
Performimg.
In the winters nights making me feel warming.
I treated her like a lady never cheating,
or misused from me you'll never feel a woman that was
scorning.
We gave each other no warnings.
Love was enormous.
High hopes of even more performance.

5. OPEN HEARTED

Open hearted.
Dearly never be departed.
Love regardless.
To me your marvelous.
I'm glad we met it started.
In my love your the main character a star.
You think with an open-mind, open hearted.

6. MORE PRECIOUS

More precious than bronze, gold medals,
silver or diamond rings, or anything.
My lady glows, gleams.
The greatness of reality,
came as a girl of my dreams.
Such a beautiful human being.
Triumphant.
Reign supreme.
For me she did anything.
More precious than silver,
bronze, gold or even
diamond rings,
or anything.

7. LOVE COMBINED

I love you more each time we combine.
Moving forward leaving our past ex's
behind.
Loved it when we kissed,
and hugged as we combined.

8. Non-Stop Love

From the bottom, center,
to the top,
the loving just wont stop.
Never decrease, never drop.
Birds of the same feather flock together
like flocks.
Father of time controls clocks,
in time love didn't wont to stop.
A reason a rhyme a love the stretches pass
distances of miles, and blocks, a love that wont stop.

9. EXCEEDED

She exceeded all expectations.
Should win the Electoral vote and run the nation.
Love permanent station.
Should be together to the end of date when the
Lord shall call us his way.
My love to keep,
my love to stay.
I can't believe we made it this far still
together right now today.

10. ORCHARD

A beautiful sight like a Red Rose
orchard of flowers.
Self empowered could never see herself
working by the hour.
A lady of power.
Stood high like a tower.
A seed that grew like a flower.
A lady of respect of great essence
of power.

93. MATTER OF FACT

Matter of fact the love we shared
shall move forward without having
to backtrack.
Love overwhelming, love overlapse.
Together we soar through the maps.
Love each season by the stack.
As a matter of fact our love shall
be together until the creator come back.

94. ONE LOVE

It's us but yet and stiil it's
one love.
We do things together as one for the love.
What's your is mines, and mines is yours,
the love.
For I am you, you are me as one,
one love.

95. THE ART OF LOVE

The art of love.
The swimming mermaid of floods.
The beautiful beauty of love.
The artwork of red hearts, red roses,
and lots of love.
The art of love.

96. Only Love For Me

Love to be.
Love that was free.
The only love for me.

LOVE VOLUME 3

1. SEPERATE

I know we seperated no longer
together, another ex I've dated.
But I still pray each day be like a holiday.
That you learn from mistakes we made.
That your new lover will be faithful,
only with you in the bed he lay.
I heard you just got married,
congratulations,
hope to agin you enjoy life,
and have lovely days.

2. ALWAYS WANTED TO BE

Where she was at I always wanted to be.
Someone I always wanted to see.
Out-going friendly.
Class and stylish personality
she had plenty.
With other men she didn't have many.
On the flip side of things I heard
she was really feeling me,
a mutual feeling
always wanted to see me.
Studied creative writing
to get a Masters Degree.
She was a writer just like me.
Somebody seem so unique,
always dressed nice hair and nails done neat.
With her is where I wanted to be.
Design for her and I together to be.

3. CAPTAIN

Captain of a ship.
Made love like a smooth sail;
a pleasurable trip.
Champagne only a little to sip.
Reframed from having a mind of filth.
Love flood strightforward, didn't tilt,
words of tips.
Kept our personal life, business,
quiet no loose lips no sanking ships.
Captain of a ship.

4. BROKEN SILENCE

She had the right to remain silence.
But she'd yell out loud the love she had in minding.
She wanted her and I to be stranded on an Island.
Someday get married and start a family.
My number she had on speed dialing.
Whatever I needed she'd go get it, findings.
What I do to stay on her mind,
she'd think all the time.
She wanted to make love to her body and my mind.
To her I was the greatest of all times.
She'd tell the crowds, and show me the love
she had in mind.

5. LOVER IN YOU

This is for, for the lover in you.
Knowing that our love will always be true.
Bright, brightness as red, yellow,
purple, and blue.
Harmonizing for you.
Always thinking of you.
Doing my best to make your
dreams come true.

This is for,
for the lover in you.

6. COURAGE AND LIGHT

Courage and light.
Wisdom and insight.
Dignity, pride, and delight.
Constant sweet dreams in the days
that turn into night.
Love letters being flown
like kites.
And this, this is the poetry I write.

7. LOVE DON'T LIVE

When it's love you don't
have to say it it'll show.
From actions to show.
I know that love don't
live here no more.
Please stop knocking
on my door.
Those you slept with those rainy nights,
winters of cold go with them go.
When I called sometimes no answer,
no text even saying hello.
Where were you when I was alone needed
a partner to hustle to flow,
no call, no show.
That's how I know love don't live, live here anymore.

8. AROUND

Around.
Love that mound.
I'm glad I found.
Love having you around.
Without me never depart town.
Love by the pounds.
Love even hearing your voice,
just sounds.
Love that goes around and around.

9. TIMELINE

Timeline of those living instead of dying.
Happiness instead of tears crying.
Visionary sight to the blind.
Freedom instead of doing time.
Making love to your mind.

10. VIEW

View love anew.
Love sky blue.
Love unto.
Love that was true.
Love me, I love you.
View.

LOVE VOLUME 4

1. LOVE WITH NO LIMIT

A love that had no limit.
Crossed the line of scrimage.
Appreciation didn't fade couldn't
deminish, it grew,
as it started from the beginning.
Hope we'd be together for life, sentenced.
We'd do it all together, good visions.
Great intentions.
Desired and progressed clearance.
Did what others wouldn't to
show love sincerest.
I love you and you love me, each other,
without a limit.

2. DURATION OF TIME

Duration of time.
Love was mines.
An everyday Valentine.
At the end of the tunnel the
light that shine.
Love all the time.
Duration of time.

3. LOVE GREW

Those that love grew.
God's chosen people a few.
Love that was like vine that grew.
Blossoming love unto.
Start as friends but grew as
a lifetime of love unto.
Love that grew.

4. BETTER

Than the rest she was better.
A trendsetter.
A love story, love letters.
Made time for those in need of
assistance to feel matter.
Gave up her own jacket
and sweater in the coldest weather.
Mind of matter.
She made me feel love it was better.

5. MORE

For you adore.
Your love I want more.
No closing of forever opened doors.
A rich love performed,
far from poor.
A galaxy universal love I adore.
Each day I love you even more.
After you I don't want to love no other woman,
no more.

6. IT'S TRUE

It's true that my love for you no-one could never undo.
Their's no me without you.
The short period of times when you're not around
I miss.
Wish I could forever kiss and hug you.
So real, so honest, so true.
It's true that I love you.

7. FIRST AND FOREMOST

First and foremost.
You are the one I love the most.
Let's be together,
live together I'm your host.
Travel from coast to coast.
Mentally a love that will
soar, will float,
holding hands never letting go.

First and foremost lets be together
even after our souls Heavenly Ghost.

First and foremost know that you
are the one I love the most.

8. DIVINE MIND

This love of life of mines.
A Cupid's arrow an everyday Valentine's.
Watch me shine.
I love you the way you do things,
and think such a divine mind.
You preached to those to stay away from
committing crimes.
Encourage people to tell the truth
instead of lying.
Left the badness gruesome past behind.
Ease minds.
Helped people get through troublesome times.
Made love to my mind.
Young in her prime but had such a divine mind.

9. GUIDANCE

Guidance.
Love and peace coinciding.
Love everlasting.
A spiritual lady
preached the word of God as food for the soul
guidance.
Roamed the streets to create peace
stop the violence.
Taught woman that they should be respected
by there mate against domestic violence.
Helped the kis with their homework to
teach knowledge wisdom understanding and guidance.
Guidance.

10. LOVE AND AFFECTION

Love and affection.
Servicing and protection.
Love confessions.
You and I together is a blessing.
Daily festival, festing.
A gift, a gem, a precious present.....
Love and affection.

LOVE VOLUME 5

1. LOVE RECEIVED

Love that was received.
Happiness achieved.
She'd swim through the Seas,
wherever I was at she wanted to be.
Love to be free.
her love to feel, to touch, to see.
She gave me everything love was and could be.

2. ADVISEMENT

An advisement.
Careful consideration of love
that was steady climbing,
steady rising.
Had to be careful of what
lies within divided.
But my love for her couldn't
be confided;
I couldn't hide it.
She made me spiritual uplifting,
uprising.
Love arising.
Seeing horizing.
Family ties.
A love I couldn't deny.

3. A Love In Mind

A love that stayed on my mind.
A love for that I could never, ever find.
A love that was of the best kind,
a visionary, a delight, supreme kind.
Sights to the blind.
Momentarily washed away problems
from minds.
Sweetest lady of past, present, and futuristic
times.
A singing sweet melody of rhymes.
Imagine living forever without dying.
A love, a love in mind.

4. DREAMED

She had a dream.
That her and I would one day say
I do, as the ring
boy handed her the ring.
That our love would be erotic,
hot as steam.
She'd pronounce me as her majesty,
her king, she'd be my queen.
Together we'd accomplish anything.
For one another do everything.
Even as we slept through the
nights together about each others
dream.

5. SPECIAL LADY OF TIMES

Fast forward.
Sometimes rewind.
Placed in with this special lady
of all times.
Fast forward so that love could excel in
due time.
Rewind until we first met,
and the sharing of pleasurable times.
I want to stay with her,
not even interested in someone
like her to find.
An intimate bind.
Stood together like a monument of holy
shrine.
This love of mines.
Our love never changed in time.
She wanted to be together for all times.
Fast forward, sometimes rewind, special lady of times.

6. WOULD LAST

Splash, remembrance of the past.
Such a blast.
I love that should've last.
The good times of smiles, and last.
It came fast.
In a blink of an eye last a flash.
The unveiling of a lovelyness on the other side of a mask.
A musical jazz.
Wish we were still together,
I wish love would've last.

7. VAST

Vast.
Love came in hurry fast.
A blast.
Abundance mass.
From a distance of vast
love came to pass.

8. BREEDER

Breeder.
Feeder.
Scripture reader.
A person for the people.
Naturally breeding.

9. NEVER CHANGED

In seasons she never changed.
But became better in time of loving
arranged.
A queen of hearts a great dame.
From her knowledge I gained.
My lady seasons, Winter, Summer, Fall,
and Spring, she never changed.

10. I Want Her Again

Again.
I want her again.
This time stay together,
love with no end.
Appreciate her to contend.
Journeys together
in life skies the limits holding
hands.
Second chance I want her again.

THIS IS LOVE VOLUME 1

1. BLACK QUEEN

The purity of love like the waters of spring.
A peaceful stream.
The emperous daughter the princess that later
became my queen.
To her our love, my life, and her loyalty to
me was everything.
Her mind stayed positive kept it clean.
In God we trust was her slogan for everything.
Together we'd celebrate, and sing.
Her love came not partially but to it's
fullest intensity, it was everything.
My beautiful black lady,
my beautiful black queen of queens.

2. ADMIRE

Admire.
Desire.
Wanna love, love to never retire.
Someday be my queen, you sire,
a castle of love free from cheating fires,
sinful desires.
Tooking higher.
Truth of love was told and showed,
without the games and falsehood of liars.
For you I love, and appreciate,
and admire.

3. BRAZIL

It was the way she made me feel.
Loving that was one hundred, the truth,
really real.
My hero, lady of steel.
Obeyed the commandments,
thou shall not cheat,
steal, or kill.
Foreign from beaches of Brazil.
My daily nutrition of a meal.
My everything in times of need a shoulder
to lean, y mind and heart is heeled.
My place of tranquil.
My lady that made me feel.
Fantastic ordeal.
My super hero,
my lady from Brazil.

4. QUALITY OF LOVE

The nourishment, quality of love I shall feed.
Aim to please indeed.
Goodness breed.
Spread wings live more, breathe.
Succeed.
Never neglect the appreciation,
value of love to be freed.....
Quality of love to feed.

5. STAY

She stayed with me throughout
the stormy weather;
after the rain came, the sun, the rainbows,
and the pot of gold, bless her soul.
A perfected woman that was the creators mold.
Turn summers out of winters cold.
A love I cherish could never let go.
A constant flow.
A female super hero.
A pro.
I truly loved her so.
For her faithfulness,
and being there for me
when it was zero below,
we shall remain lovers
even in the days of old.

6. LOVING, FREE

The cool breeze.
Soft winds that blow with ease.
The blossoming of flowers and trees.
My love to please.
Pleasurable sights to see.
To the fullest extent, highest degree.
Loving, freely the way it suppose to be.
Free.

7. TWIST

Refreshing with a twist.
Love that had no secret agenda,
no hidded motive,
but instead a bliss.
Luscious lips to kiss.
My female knight in shining armor,
the best as it gets.
Creative in details of how she would
make our love stand as it sits.
My lady of time, my lady historical events.
A love that's pure, and refreshing with a
lovely twist.

8. ESTABLISHED

Established.
Love above, and beyond average.
Gave me a crown, just for me made her home
a palace.
Told me I had a gift continue to pursue
my dreams my unforbidden talent.
Lovely poems, lovely sonnets, well proposed ballets.
She wanted us to be together each second, each minute,
through the days, years that came from hours.
Didn't want anything from me but love, appreciation,
and the golden grain of it's powers.
She had everything else she needed,
she already was established.

9. My Sun That Shine

My sun shine.
This light of mine let it shine,
let it shine.
Forever be mine.
Shine even when I feel in the blind
left behind;
When I need love all the time.
Shine even in the grimness of the night time.
Shine only for me be mines,
faithful throughout this and even next lifetime.
This light sunny lady of mines,
let ti shine.

10. TOGETHER

Lets stay together.
Spend each night and day together.
Lay together.
Pray together.
Loving whenever.
Cut from the same cloth,
birds of the same feather.
Seems to me loving just
don't get any better.

Loving always, and forever.
Stay, let's stay together.

THIS IS LOVE VOLUME 2

1. THE TRUTH

She is the truth.
Love, respect, and everlasting appreciation
is always due.
My heart of love of my soul unto.
You are a reflection of me,
and I'm a reflection of you to.
Skies are blue, always when loving you.
Abided by the scriptures in the King James
versions to.
The path of honesty, loyalty righteous was,
and is within you.
You've seen it all,
to you nothing under the sun was new.
No fictional stories are false advertising for you,
kept it real, being yourself, you are the truth.

2. LOVELY DAYS

Lovely days.
Loving in special ways.
Sun shine their way.
Shall be together forever and a day.
Wedding bells ring,
vows was made;
later on the blessing that was gave
as the seeded children were made.
As kids joyfully play.
Nothing but love songs and poetry conveyed.....
Lovely days.

3. AVANT

So wonderful, so beautiful, from spacious skies,
from every mountain top.
Convenant of love of avant.
Soothing love I never want it to stop.

4. GOD'S BABY

She sat teary eyes,
shedding tears visions hazy.
She'd pray for the Haitians in Haiti.
Gob bless the child,
God bless the men, the boys,
the girls, the babies,
and ladies,
lord please provide food, and shelter
lord please save thee.

She wasn't interested in other men,
she loved me like crazy.
Went to work seven days a week, even holidays,
never lazy.
True essence of God's child,
one of God's babies.

God bless the child that got it's own.
God bless the babies.

5. MAKE RIGHT

In life make things right.
Like a diamond shine so bright.
Hungry for success as a daily appetite.
Stay focus throughout stormy days,
and cold nights.
Make, life right.

6. GIFT OF LIFE

The gift that keeps on giving.
Being a product of livilyhood of living.
We are God's children.
Healthy babies being born,
life is for the giving.
Gift of life,
worth living.

7. Golden Eagle Fly Away

Golden Eagle,
the sunlight of morning chirping birds.
Fly, fly far away to see, live to be fruitful,
to see a bigger, and brighter day.
Allowing the Lord to have things his way.
Never letting pleasant memories fade.
Be a positive product of what our father made.

Fly, fly far away where your presence is a gift,
and others always want you to stay.
Love even when skies are grey.

Fly, fly far away where the happiness of space will evade,
parades showering of lovely days.

8. INDEPENDENCE

She declared independence.
Foreign but became a U.S. citizen.
She gave everything, to her life was for the giving.
Didn't depend on a man she went out worked to get it,
Ms. Independent.
Had no kids, decided to wait to she was married to have children.
Despised men that created domestic violence
against women.
To her dating me was an honor, and privilege.
For us together happy she pursued it with relentless.
She prayed for freedom for those that had been wrongfully
convicted.
She'd stress to everyone to think wisely and make wise decisions.
She was inspiration, a gift,
an everyday Christmas.

She declared independence,
without her my days of happiness
would have no existence.

9. STARS AND MOONS

Stars and the moons, became one with the sun.
Love had just begun.
The shining even in the darkest night like
the enchanting array that comes from the summer sun.
Someday shall be my spouse birth my first son.
I wonder why the creator blessed me with your love,
your life, the excitement, enjoyment, the loving, the fun.
As the stars, the moon, and the sun became one.

10. Giving Chance

In advance she gave love a chance.
Made me feel like a king, a man.
Romance.
Grand stand.
My biggest fan.
Love in advance, giving chance.

THIS IS LOVE VOLUME 3

1. HEAVENLY FATHER FORGIVE

Heavenly father forgive us for sins,
and fears.
Heavenly father allow us to live
throughout the years.
Heavenly father please whip away all our blood sweat,
and tears.

2. FILL

Fill me with the tenderness of your
touch.
Let's move slow don't rush.
Let's be as a holy spirit to lust.
In God we trust.

Fill me with the tenderness of your touch.

3. CHANGING DURATION

In the morning I'll be your eastern, sunrise,
sunshine.

In the evening I'll be your lover for pleasuring
pleasing.

In the night will make everything nice, and right.

4. ACTION

In action.
Climaxing, and everlasting satisfaction.
Love lasting.
Gratifying.
Each other satisfying.

5. LOVE KNOWS

Love knows.
Love grows.
Love continue to flow.

6. SHE WAS

She was my lady of light,
shine so bright.

She was my majestic queen
To me she meant the world everything.

She my female knight in shining
armor, she lovely and marvelous.

7. THE VERY ESSENCE

Essence of time.
Love to my soul, and mind.
Loved her grace, love her kind.

Essence of time.

8. In Life The Love

In life the love came from up above.
An angel she was.
Spreaded her wings for love.
Lovely in love.....
In life she gave nothing but love.

9. ZODIAC

Capricon, native American, native born.
Gemini, for I am you, you are I.
Scorpio, there was no better love I'd known before.
Leo, female super hero.
Cancer, a great friend, lovely romancer.

10. FATE

Love making.
Congratulating.
Awaiting.
Anticipating.
Keeping the faith.
Together with fate.

11. SOME I WANT

Her, she that will always choose me first.
Share our love for what it was worth.
When I'm sick be my nurse.
When I'm worried pray with me to take
away pain that hurts.
Seeded lady that gave birth.
Love me for richer or poor, better or worse.
If I perish first love me still six feet
under the dirt.

12. LORD OF LORDS

Lord of Lords.
King of Kings.
The inventor of life shining light that gleams.
Master of the day of judgement supreme.
Reflection of as kings and queens.
God of all things.
My lord of lords,
my king of kings.

13. COME

Come closer.
Allow love to runneth over.
Together we grow older, closer.
Come to me, come closer.

THIS IS LOVE VOLUME 4

1. SLICK RHYMES

Rhymes that will allow mankind to shine.
Enhance desires design.
Rhymes that will keep peace in minds.
Rhymes knowing that it's love all the time.

2. LOVING YOU FOREVER

Loving you forever is what I need.
Proceed breathe, achieve.
Indeed.
Loving you forever is all I need.

3. TOGETHER, RATHER

Let's stay together rather happy or
sad good and bad.
To have you I'm proud I'm glad.
The best love I ever had loving you forever
rather times are good or bad.

4. HOLD YOUR HEAD

Hold up hold your head up.
Reach for it grab it grab the sky.
Worship honor respect the most high,
hold your head up to the sky.

5. BETTER OR WORSE

For better or worse I'll choose you first.
Love that begin at birth.
No sins for seeds to be curse.
For better or worse I'll always choose you first.
Lovely love being dispursed.

6. RED ROSE

Red Rose I love seeing you as I awake to open my eyes
as I dream eyes closed.
Love you more than you can imagine,
more than you know.
Love to grow.
Blossoming as the sunshine,
the cool breeze tenderness as the wind blow.
Love you more, love to grow.

7. ALWAYS

Always on my mind.
Lovely and divine.
Aged better in time.
Another you I can't find.
Always on time always in my mind.

8. She Was A Blessing

Learned lessons.
She was a blessing.
She better than the rest.
She was my havon my love soul
through the flesh.
She was everything she was blessed.

9. LOVELY DREAMS.

Of you I have sweet dreams.
A wake up in the morning,
seeing your face that gleams.
The woman of my dreams.
The reality of everything.
All things I ever wanted came through my queen.

10. LOVE EVERLASTING

Love everlasting.
Satisfying.
A height of above the cloud
love no denying.
Eternal defying.
Love everlasting through timely fashion.

THIS IS LOVE VOL 5

1. LADY FOREVER

Can we be together forever throughout the seasons,
of changing weathers.
Love at it's best that can't get any better.
Solid like a stone, Rosetta.
My rose, my Lavender, my feather.
My lady of today, and tomorrow, my lady forever.

2. BEST OF HER

She allowed me to inherit the best of her.
The all and the rest of her.
A leisure of the loveliest pleasure.
Hidden treasures.
The best of her in unrated,
presidential measures.
couldn't get no better.
Loving together, whenever.
The best of her I desire forever.

3. LOVING REGARDLESS

Loving regardless.
Marvelous.
Special and stardon.
To her my imperfection didn't bother.
Sweet heart, darling.
Didn't complain about problems.
Us going down the aisle to the alter
was her plan, target.
A red ribbon of contemporary enlargement.
Loved me no matter what regardless.

4. A LOVE

A love in which the creator design.
You stay on my mind.
The best of your kind.
The greatest of all time.
Times of dispair apart,
I think daily you always on my mind.

5. 24/7

Treat her like Heaven.
24/7.
Making her always feel delightful,
and pleasant.
Love as a cherishable, daily gift, present.
Treat her like Heaven 24/7.

6. SMILE

I love to see you smile all the while.
My lovely lady, my Godle child.
For I'll do what it takes to make you smile.
Love all the while.
My emperess of time filed.
I love to see you smile.

7. CENTER

Center of my only true love.
Center of my attraction.
Love everlasting.
Center my world, my satisfaction.

8. BARE WITNESS

I bare witness that there was love for the giving,
and she gave.
My daily parade of sunny days shining my way.
Love was made, love was gave.
Lovely days.

9. HER, I, WE

In the beginning til the end,
there was her she us we.
Love to be.
Love that was free.
Love that flowed,
like purity of streams.

10. Her Eyes (Alexus)

I can always stare into her pretty browm eyes,
and see the sunrise.
Heavenly peace within her eyes.
Through her I shall live forever even after
I pass in a fashionable timely demise.
When you was a baby I'd whip away tears from eyes;
Red don't cry.
I thank the Heavenly Father for your life
that came alive.
To the end bitter end for you I shall ride.
I know you may not see me from time to time,
but I'm on the road doing shows,
a constant grind, so later on in life they'll
be no struggle,
we shall overcome, we shall shine.
Love you all the time.
Whatever I own is yours and mines.
Forever soaring through the clouds of time.
Through you N'dia and Asia was brought alive,
my descendants another one of mine.

I look into your pretty brown eyes and see family ties,
new borns being baptize,
and my future being prosperous with achievements of enterprise.

I can see it in your eyes.

Printed in the United States
By Bookmasters